THE HISTORY OF JAPAN

Other Books by

KENNETH SCOTT LATOURETTE

A SHORT HISTORY OF THE FAR EAST

THE CHINESE : THEIR HISTORY AND CULTURE

The

HISTORY *of* JAPAN

By KENNETH SCOTT LATOURETTE

*Sterling Professor of Missions and Oriental History, Emeritus, and
Associate Fellow of Berkeley College in Yale University*

Revised Edition

NEW YORK

THE MACMILLAN COMPANY

1957

Revised edition of a work originally published under the title The
Development of Japan.

Sixth Printing, 1963

CONTENTS

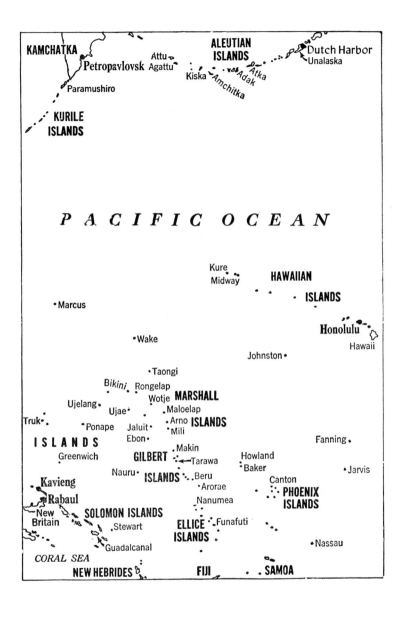

THE HISTORY OF JAPAN

CHAPTER I

THE GEOGRAPHIC SETTING OF JAPAN

Until August, 1945, Japan occupied most of the islands which stretch along the eastern coast of Asia from Kamchatka to the southern end of the Malay Peninsula. Her possessions reached from the northernmost of the Kurile Islands (Chishima), south of Kamchatka, to the southern cape of Formosa (called Taiwan by the Japanese), a distance of about twenty-five hundred miles and equal to the distance from Cuba to Newfoundland. The islands held numbered over three thousand and had a total area of 173,786 square miles, or a little more than that of the state of California. They are about twice the size of the British Isles. Most of the islands are very small and only about six hundred are inhabited. The six principal ones are Hokkaido (Yezo), Honshu, the so-called Main Island where Japan's six largest cities are located, Shikoku, Kyushu and until 1945, Sakhalin (Karafuto), and Formosa (Taiwan). Hokkaido was until recently inhabited chiefly by the Ainu, a primitive people. It has since been rapidly developed by the Japanese. Honshu alone comprises over half the entire area of the island part of the empire. On it from the earliest historic times has been the center of government. Shikoku, "The Four Provinces," derives its name from an ancient administrative division of the island, and forms part of the southern border of the Inland Sea, famous for the beauties of its waters, islands, and shores. Kyushu is literally "The Nine Provinces," a designation also derived from an earlier gov ernmental organization. It is separated from Honshu by the narrow straits of Shimonoseki, through which passes most of the shipping from the east coast of Asia to North America. Kyushu is a comparatively short distance from Korea, and since it is also nearer to China than any other of the principal islands of the older Japan, it was the gateway through which came most of the influences from the continent. Kyushu was the first island to be greatly affected by intercourse with Europe in the sixteenth century. Its chief port, industrial Nagasaki, is still one of the most important harbors in the empire. Formosa was ceded to Japan by China in 1895 and racially was never assimilated into the rest of the nation. To the north of Karafuto lie the Kurile Islands, which are a long line of thinly settled islands. Kyushu and Formosa are connected by the Ryukyu group, which has become definitely Japanese only within the past seventy years. In addition to its islands, until her defeat in 1945, during part of the present century Japan held the neighboring peninsula of Korea (Chosen) which has about half the area of the island part of the empire, and dominated the adjoining territories of Manchuria (Manchukuo), Inner Mongolia, and the northeastern and eastern provinces of China proper. Of these possessions more will be said later. Japan also acquired the former German island possessions in the Pacific north of the equator at the close of World War I.

THE EFFECTS OF GEOGRAPHY UPON THE JAPANESE PEOPLE AND THEIR HISTORY

But this account of its main component parts and area reveals little of the many important effects that the land has had upon its people. First of all, the fact that the historic Japan has been a closely associated group of islands has promoted unity. As we shall see later, the Japanese, although of diverse origin, are a distinct type, and have, with the exception of a few sections in the north and in the newly acquired islands in the south, attained a remarkable similarity. They have as well a highly developed national consciousness. Their intense patriotism has undoubtedly been furthered by the fact that the sea has separated them from other peoples. Prior to 1945 the islands had never been successfully invaded since the original migrations of the ancestors of the Japanese. Only during the great Mongol irruptions in the thirteenth century was the nation seriously threatened with foreign rule. In the past the invasions that succeeded have been those of ideas, not of peoples. The civilization that has grown up, although deeply affected by influences from without, has been Japanese. The free and at times wholesale borrowing of foreign cultures has always been marked by a characteristic originality that has put a Japanese stamp on all that has been acquired.

Then the fact that the Japanese are an island people has encouraged them to become a sea-faring folk. This tendency has been strengthened by the large number of protected bays and the absence of great gaps between islands. The harbors at Nagasaki and Yokohama, to mention only two, are among the best in the world. The Sea of Japan, dotted with islands, free from storms, and near the home of early Japanese civilization, invited to a life on the water. The Japanese have been famous fishermen. It is but natural that in this age of international commerce they developed a large merchant fleet.

The Japanese islands have, moreover, a peculiarly close relation to the eastern shore of Asia. Their nearness to the coast promotes relations. In at least three places they have nearly touched the continent, so communication has been comparatively easy — Sakhalin on the north, Kyushu and Korea in the center, and Formosa on the south. Of greatest importance has been the second, for it was partly through Korea that the ancestors of the Japanese reached the islands.

It was through Korea that the main stream of Chinese and Indian culture flowed to Japan. It was through Korea that commercial intercourse with the continent most easily took place. Through Karafuto may have come some primitive tribes from the north, possibly the ancestors of the modern Ainu. Through Formosa by way of the Ryukyu Islands Malay elements entered, and possibly some strains of blood from the mainland.

This nearness to Asia means, too, that the Japanese have been vitally interested in affairs of the mainland. They saw there a natural field for commercial and territorial expansion. There too was a possible outlet for their surplus population. They have tried to prevent strong foreign powers from dominating the points where Japan most nearly touches Asia. Hence they fought both Russia and China for Korea, and later annexed it. Hence they demanded that China permit no European power to control the coast of Fuhkien province opposite Formosa. They have also insisted that their voice be heard in settling the affairs of China, and that her door be kept open to their commerce. They attempted during World War I so to establish themselves in the great Asiatic republic that they could not be easily dislodged when the struggle should be over. In short, the Japanese intended to make themselves supreme on the mainland of Asia and to shut out, so far as possible, other foreign nations.

The length of the chain of islands, combined with the nearness to the coast of Asia, has been a factor of importance. In prehistoric days it meant that from many different points different racial elements could find their way into the islands. Thus through Karafuto have come peoples akin to those of Siberia, through Korea various folk from Central Asia, China, and Korea, and from the south some of Malay blood. In more recent times this relationship to the continent has placed Japan in a position to control nearly all the east coast

The relation of Japan to the mainland of Asia

of Asia. Great Britain because of her location was able to control the ocean routes to northwestern Europe and to be queen of the North Atlantic; even more does Japan's geographical position enable her to exert wide control over the foreign commerce and shipping of far-eastern Asia.

Their location made the Japanese the first interpreters of the culture of the Occident, that is, of Europe and America, to the Far East   It is no mere accident that Japan should have been the first nation of that region unreservedly to unbar her doors to the West. Her great harbors, some facing Asia and some America, were an open challenge to the Western world when the age of steam began to dot the Pacific with ships. Nor is it an accident that Japan should have led in opening Korea, and that Chinese should have flocked in such numbers to her universities to acquire the new learning. For geographical reasons Japan has believed herself destined to guide the Far East into the new age.

Not only have her island position and her relation to the Asiatic mainland influenced Japan greatly, but the characteristics of the land itself have been important. In the first place, the islands are very mountainous. They are badly broken by peaks and ranges. Some of these are of volcanic origin, others the result of folding, but they occupy the larger part of Japan's surface. As a result only a small part of the land can be cultivated. At present about seventeen per cent of Japan's area (exclusive of Korea) is listed as farmland. Probably another ten per cent can be reclaimed, although the process will prove costly. This means that the limits of population supported by home-grown food are soon reached. Any excess beyond these limits must either emigrate or busy itself, as in Great Britain, with manufacturing and commerce. There is near at hand, however, a vast continent. In Manchuria, Mongolia, and Siberia are unoccupied lands for immigrants. In China there is a teeming, industrious population, one of the greatest potential markets in the world, and unmeasured supplies of raw material.

Mt. Aso, the largest active volcano in Japan

Nearly the entire eastern coast of Asia is a great grain-producing region and is to become a greater one. Moreover, the mountains of Japan invite manufacturing as they are in places well stocked with coal, and their streams can be harnessed to provide water power. They are lacking in iron ore, but this is found in some abundance in China proper and Manchuria, not far from navigable streams which connect directly with the sea and with Japan. Japan insisted that the door on the neighboring continent be kept open to her, and it is true that she sought special privileges there. Here was a source of food; here was a possible outlet for surplus population; here was a market for her manufactures; here a store of raw materials. Japan wanted all these things.

The mountains cut the islands into small valleys and plains. There are few navigable streams, and in the old days before the advent of railways, telegraphs, and steamboats, intercommunication was difficult. As in most mountain countries the nation separated naturally into small groups, each of which tended to become independent of the central power, and the feudal form of government and the emphasis on family which we are later to notice easily developed.

Japan is favored in climate. She lies largely in the temperate zone, the home of the great civilizations of the globe. She is said to have, more than any other country of Asia, cyclonic disturbances which help to produce the marked changes in temperature from day to day that are believed to promote human activity and civilization. She has an abundant rainfall. The Black Current, a warm ocean stream from the tropics, washes a portion of her shores. Vegetation is luxurious and as much of her land as is tillable responds splendidly to the efforts of the farmer. Her large population could not have been self-supporting for so long had soil and climate not been favorable.

The natural surroundings may, moreover, partly account for the love of beauty that has been associated with the Japanese. The wooded hills, the infinite variety of mountain and valley, of lake and harbor and sea, could not have failed to develop in some of the people a sense of the artistic. The land is one of the most beautiful in the world, and the inhabitants have responded to it with a love for flowers, for trees, for birds, for moonlit lakes, for streams and waterfalls.

Mt. Fuji is a symbol of the country.

The location and the natural resources and characteristics of the islands, then, have had and still have a strong influence upon the people, their civilization, their ambitions, and their policies.

CHAPTER II

From the Earliest Times to the Introduction of Buddhism

Of the early history of the Japanese we have an imperfect record. Traditions, myths, and fragments of poetry and religious ritual have told us something. Ethnology (the study of the races of mankind) and archeology (the study of relics and remains) are telling us a little more. The most ancient written records now in existence did not take their present form until the eighth century A.D. The myths and traditions as they have come down to us give a most childlike account of the origin of the land, the people, and the state. Curious and numerous gods and goddesses are seen.

The complete story of these early centuries is a long one, but the many attempts that have been made to find in it traces of true history disclose only a minimum of fact. According to the story taught in Japan, the emperor is descended from the gods, and the imperial house follows "a lineal succession unbroken for ages eternal." Hirohito became by Japanese reckoning the 123rd of these rulers. The belief helps to invest the ruling line with divine dignity. The Japanese peoples, moreover, at the time of Perry's coming (1853), believed they, too, were descended from the gods and so superior to other people, and the land was held to be the country of the gods. Of all the earth Japan was nearest to heaven when the connection between the two was broken. While never so generally nor so strongly held as the belief in the divine origin of the emperor, these convictions produced an attitude of mind that may still reënforce the intense patriotism that is typical of the Japanese.

From these stories, reënforced by ethnology and archeology, it seems that the earliest inhabitants of the islands were a race called "cave men." Their very existence is questioned. If they were a real people, the only remaining traces of them are pit dwellings and shell mounds, and they must have been in the most primitive stages of culture. Entirely historical, however, are a strong race of primitive folk, probably the ancestors of those Ainu who are still to be found on the island of Hokkaido and the Kurile Islands. They are hairy, flat-faced people and rather mild-tempered. Of their origin nothing certain is known; some have supposed that they came from northern Asia. When the first Japanese found their way to the islands these primitive people were in possession of most of the land. Then they were a fierce lot, still in the stone age. They were cannibals, and apparently were without family life. They offered a sturdy resistance to the more nearly civilized invaders and were driven back and subdued only after long centuries of warfare, warfare which continued to within the past few hundred years. They left permanent marks on their conquerors, chiefly in an admixture of blood which is strongest in the north.

The Japanese of today are a mixed race and are the result of the fusion of several migrations. We cannot trace with certainty all the streams, but there must have been several of them from various sources, reaching the islands at different times. The blending of these groups has never been entirely completed. From the earliest times there have been two pronounced types, the aristocratic, slender of limb and of light complexion, and the common people, stocky and dark. The migrations came from the continent for the most part, chiefly by the way of the Korean Peninsula, but also from the south. There are strong strains of Malay blood which are apparently due to settlements partly from the continent and partly from the southern islands. Too little is as yet known of the origin of the Far Eastern peoples to enable us to determine accurately all the racial connections of the Japanese. Manchu-Korean and Malay stocks predominate, but there are as well traces of infusion of other blood, part of it Mongol, part of it probably Chinese, and part of it still undetermined.

When they arrived in the islands some of the ancestors of the Japanese were in the bronze age and some in the iron age. They were evidently much superior to, although probably less numerous than the original inhabitants whom they found in possession. The time of the foundation of the Japanese state was probably several hundred years later than the legendary 660 B.C. Its center was at Yamato. Extension was not an easy matter; it was achieved only through constant warfare with other Japanese, and against the ancestors of the Ainu, who stubbornly contested every foot of ground.

THE YAMATO STATE

The culture of the little kingdom that centered at Yamato was primitive enough. There were no cities and no carefully constructed houses. For several centuries writing was either unknown or used only by a very few. The land was owned principally by the emperors and the noble families. There was some navigation in small craft, and fish formed a part of the national diet, although probably not so largely as now. Rice and other grains were cultivated. Many kinds of vegetables were known and used. The dense forests that originally covered the land were gradually cleared away, and tilled fields took their places. Irrigation was practiced. Game was hunted in the forests and formed a part of the diet. Food was cooked in unglazed earthen vessels. For clothing, silk was used a little, but the principal fabrics were made from hemp and bark. Cotton was not introduced from China until later and wool was unknown. There was no money and such trade as existed was carried on by barter. Art was crude, although, contrary to the custom of later ages, the

A typical farm home of a hard-working Japanese   *Keystone Photo*

Japanese elaborately decked themselves with personal ornaments. Some of the war equipment showed the beginnings of artistic design.

There were a few simple trades, for implements were needed on the farm, in the home, and for battle. Skilled workers were organized by guilds. Life was largely agricultural and military. The population was divided into a number of different classes; serfs were to be found, and slavery existed, as might be expected from the constant warfare. There were apparently no codes of law, and justice was administered in a crude kind of way. The accused frequently swore to his innocence before the gods and as proof of guilt-lessness thrust his arm in boiling water or carried a hot iron in his hand. Customs that seem to us cruel were in use. For example, the servants, wives, and secondary wives, or concubines, of a chief were buried alive by the grave of their lord. Not until later, and then probably due to influence from the continent, were clay images substituted for the living sacrifices.

From the beginning the state was based on war, and the prolonged struggle with the Ainu and provinces in the south and west but tended to emphasize this characteristic. Unlike the Chinese, their Asiatic neighbors, the Japanese as they expanded were compelled to fight for every inch of soil. As a result their culture had largely a military as well as an agricultural cast. In China the soldier has usually been considered of secondary importance, an evil to be endured only because he is necessary for the defense of the scholars, farmers, and merchants. In Japan, with the exception of a few important centuries, the soldier has controlled the state.

The power of the emperor apparently dates from the earliest days of the nation. That does not mean that it was originally what it became more recently. It was a gradual growth. At first the ruler was simply the leader who united the various tribes or families in war and formed a unified center in the intervals of peace. Theoretically, possibly as a result of the unity made necessary by the long warfare with the original settlers and other enemies, he was in complete control; practically he shared his power with local chieftains, and the state resembled a federation of tribes under his hereditary leadership. Not all the chieftains were loyal. Those in the far west and south were often virtually independent and gave allegiance to the Yamato court only when a strong monarch sat on the throne. The emperor was high priest, and declared war and peace. The Japanese people never lost their faith in him. When the great transformation of the nineteenth century came, the emperor became the rallying point for the reorganized nation.

Religion was simple. There was no formal church or organized priesthood and no elaborate system of ethics.

Philip Gendreau, N. Y.

Rice farming in Japan depends on ankle-deep water and strong backs.

Their ideas of the origin of the world were childlike. The people had not yet thought deeply on conduct, or on the mysteries of life and the origin of things. The great forces and objects of nature were given godlike qualities and the spirits of ancestors were worshipped, especially those of the imperial house: religion came to be, in fact, very largely the spirit and backbone of the royal power. Man was believed to be surrounded by a host of spirits who lived in trees, or rocks, or the air. Animals as well as men might be regarded as divinities. Shrines were few in number and crude in architecture. Ritual was not elaborate or complicated, and consisted largely in adoration and satisfaction of spirits, gods, and ancestors, and in purification from ceremonial uncleanness. This purification was partly associated with a personal cleanliness which seems then as now to have been a national characteristic. In common with other primitive peoples various objects were held to be taboo, a corpse, for example, and a woman at childbirth. This primitive religion has persisted with amazingly few changes. Originally it had no distinctive name, but after foreign cults entered, it became self-conscious and was named Shinto, "the Way of the Gods." Present-day Shintoism is this primitive religion with the changes that it has undergone through the centuries.

The simple culture here described was the product of centuries through which progress was taking place and changes were always occurring. Only dimly can we picture these times, and even more inadequately can we treat them in a book of this length.

CHINESE CIVILIZATION: ITS CONTACT WITH JAPAN

While the Japanese state was growing up around Yamato, a mighty civilization was being formed in nearby Asia. Beginning at least as early as 2000 B.C., in what is now the northwestern section of China proper, the Chinese people had been increasing in numbers and territory, and by about A.D. 200, they had produced a philosophy, a literature, an art, and an industrial and commercial organization that compare favorably with the best cultures of Greece or Rome. Confucius had meditated on the philosophy, ethics, and statecraft of China, and from them developed a group of writings and sayings, the major part of the so-called Chinese classics. These have had an influence on a larger proportion of mankind than any other literary collection outside of the Christian and the Buddhist scriptures.

Writing in China had been brought to a high state of perfection in the form of characters, partly phonograms (sounds expressed in graphic characters), partly ideographs, partly pictographs, and a literary form had been produced which with remarkably few alterations is the standard for the Chinese written language to-day. Agriculture, industry, and commerce flourished. Population had multiplied. This expanding culture on the neighboring continent naturally affected Japan. Chinese rulers of the Han dynasty (B.C. 206–A.D. 214) had set themselves over part of Korea and the civilization they brought with them made itself felt in the Yamato state. In the centuries that followed Japanese embassies were sent to the court of China. Much that was Chinese was adopted by the semi-barbarous islanders; writing was introduced, although the knowledge of it made headway but slowly, and Confucian philosophy became known in court circles. Korean and Chinese skilled workers and merchants migrated at times in large numbers, bent upon developing for their own profit the market afforded by the eager, virile, backward Japanese. With them, as with the Western merchants of later centuries, came a civilization which the Japanese borrowed and stamped with their own characteristic imprint.

This contact between China and Japan continued for several centuries and under its influence Japanese culture had been slowly developing, when a series of events took place which within a few years was to work a transformation in the island kingdom. The Chinese race was expanding. For centuries it was divided into petty states, but a renewed unity came and was followed by further expansion and a flowering of art and literature which profoundly affected all eastern Asia including Japan. The vehicle for this enlarged contribution of culture from China to Japan was Buddhism.

CHAPTER III

FROM THE INTRODUCTION OF BUDDHISM (A.D. 552) TO THE
ORGANIZATION OF THE SHOGUNATE (A.D. 1192)

THE ORIGIN, DEVELOPMENT, AND SPREAD OF BUDDHISM

Buddhism began in northern India in the sixth century before Christ as a reforming movement and a protest against the religious system of the time. Its founder was Gautama (usually known as Gautama Buddha), a man of noble blood, who after years of inner struggle had found peace of mind and had endeavored to transmit his secret to others. Sharing the beliefs of his times, he taught that life was a long chain of reincarnations or rebirths, and that it meant poverty, suffering, disease, and death. Suffering, he had discovered, was caused by men's desires and longings. To get rid of it one must get rid of desire. The stage at which one reached the perfect elimination of desire was called Nirvana, and when it was reached the chain of reincarnations with their bringing of suffering was broken. This victory over desire was to be achieved by a combination of methods whose chief practical emphasis was upon a life of meditation, self-sacrifice, and unselfish service. The material world was temporary, and man was to learn to think of its goods as a delusion and to free himself from all longing for them. As Gautama taught it, Buddhism had little to say about the gods. If they existed they were subject to change and would pass away, and had best be ignored. Man could achieve salvation by his own strength unaided by the divine.

After Gautama's death his system underwent a change.

were imported; architecture became prominent for the first time. Buddhist temples were erected on the model of those on the continent, marked contrasts to the simple buildings that had done for the Shinto worship and the flimsy structures in which even royalty had lived. Inspired by the construction of temples, better and more permanent dwellings were erected for the emperor and the nobility.

Various handicrafts were introduced from Korea and China and the Japanese became familiar with new utensils and implements, with better textiles and industrial methods. Chinese medicine and military science were brought in. The Chinese calendar was formally adopted. Chinese costumes were introduced, and their use and form carefully regulated by law. Roads were built, probably for the first time. Communication by land now supplemented that by boats, heretofore the chief means of transportation. Shipbuilding was improved and commerce grew. A system of weights and measures was adopted. The importation of the precious metals stimulated the Japanese to open mines of their own. Silver was discovered in the islands and shortly afterward, copper. With the working of native ores came the minting of money. In the early years of the eighth century the first true coins were struck. They were mostly of copper as in China.

There was also an immigration of Koreans and Chinese into Japan. Some were Buddhist missionaries, drawn partly by zeal and partly by ambition. Some were handicraftsmen. Others were merchants who were interested in exploiting the resources of the newly opened islands. Still others were scholars, attracted by the rewards offered by the court and the nobility for men of learning.

There were great social changes. Wealth increased and with it the difference between rich and poor became more apparent. A greater emphasis was laid upon agriculture.

The Japanese family was modified and strengthened by contact with Chinese ideals, which were, briefly, that orderly family life and its attendant reverence for ancestors are the basis of society.

THE POLITICAL CHANGES DUE TO CONTACT WITH CHINA AND THE CONTINENT

Especially noteworthy was the reorganization which took place in the state. Prince Shotoku, a strong advocate of Buddhism, was equally in favor of the new culture. He was a student not only of Buddhism, but of the great historic classics of China, the writings of Confucius and his school, and was an eager and intelligent admirer of Chinese government. It was due partly to his influence that a complete reorganization of the Japanese government took place. In 604 he issued his "constitution" in seventeen articles, sometimes called Japan's first written code of laws. This was not an elaborate legal document listing specific crimes and prescribing penalties, but an attempt to apply in a somewhat general way Buddhist and Confucian moral principles to official life. It was a body of moral rules sent out as instructions to the leaders of the state to guide them in the performance of their duties. Reverence for Buddhism and loyalty to the emperor were insisted upon, a high standard of personal uprightness was encouraged, and justice and integrity were commanded in the fulfillment of public duty. After the death of Shotoku, a complete reorganization of the state took place. Additional reforms followed under succeeding monarchs for over a period of nearly a century.

The changes made during these years, consisting mainly in an attempt to adapt to Japan the governmental system of China, were formulated in the Taikwa Reforms. The process was revolutionary and not altogether successful. China was a great agricultural, industrial, and commercial state whose

organization rested on an absolute monarch through a body
of officials carefully chosen by competitive civil service
examinations. The government existed in theory for the
good of the people and was interested in everything per-
taining to their welfare. Now, the Japanese were a military
and an agricultural folk. Their state was small and was made
up of a number of provinces under local chieftains. They
loosely acknowledged the leadership of an hereditary ruler
who was supposed to be descended from the gods. The
attempt was made to reproduce in this very foreign setting
a political organization which had been developed to meet
an entirely different set of needs. In 784 the seat of government was transferred to a new site, the present Kyoto, and
a new and larger city was built. This was the home of the
emperors until the nineteenth century.

The outstanding feature of the new government was the
increase in the power of the Japanese monarch. His position
already had much of sacredness attached to it. (Jimmu
Tenno, the first emperor, was believed to be a descendant
of the Sun Goddess, the divine ancestress of all the Japanese
people.) The ruler became even more commanding, the
source of all authority. Rebellion against the throne was
held to be a crime against religion. A change of dynasty
would have been utterly contrary to the ideas established in
the people's minds.

A division between civil and military officials was made.
No longer were the duties of the soldier and the adminis-
trator to be combined as in the earlier days. Then the nation
was, in many respects, a collection of tribes and families
rather loosely united by allegiance to the royal house. Now
a sharp division of duties was introduced on the model of the
system in use in China. A governing body of civil officials
was created and these were to be chosen partly on the basis
of noble blood, and partly by means of civil-service examina-

tions based largely on the classics of Confucius. Capacity for administration was thus measured, as on the continent, by the ability to produce an elegant and learned essay in Chinese. To prepare candidates, schools were established in the capital and the provinces. A central ministry of eight departments was organized. Codes of laws were issued, inspired by Chinese models. The attempt was made to insure justice for all. Although the old noble families were retained, many of the existing social gradations were abolished, and a new division of classes was introduced. All Japanese, regardless of rank, were to be subject to the emperor and to his courts and his laws. Any might freely petition the monarch for righting of wrongs. Military conscription was introduced, again under the influence of the continent. From a third to a fourth of the able-bodied citizens were to be in the service at one time.

All the soil was now held by the emperor. A few families had previously controlled most of the land, reducing the mass of the rural population to a condition resembling serfdom, and threatening the power of the crown. State ownership was now asserted, the land was redivided, and each man and woman was given a share. To prevent the soil from being seized again by a few landowners and to allow for the growth of population, a redistribution of the fields was to take place every six years. Tracts of land were allotted to officials, whose salaries were to be paid by the income from their estates and not by taxing the peasants. Forced labor was reorganized and work was to be partly exchanged for taxes in farm produce. Since the Japanese still occupied only a part of the surface of the islands, expansion was encouraged by granting a larger degree of private ownership in lands acquired through reclamation. The system of taxation was made over: officials were for the most part exempt, but an effort was made to effect a uniform levy upon the people at large.

The entire population was divided, somewhat on Chinese lines, into groups made up of five households each, and into larger units of fifty households. These groups were for purposes of police and mutual defense. The collective responsibility of a group for the conduct of each of its members was insisted upon and the criminal code of China was taken over, although in a modified form. For more than a century it was the standard by which Japanese cases were tried.

The modification of national life under the influence of the mainland was the main factor in Japan's history from the middle of the sixth to late in the eighth century. It recurred, although at long intervals and with less prominence, until the coming of the Europeans in the nineteenth century. Every new burst of culture in China made itself felt in Japan during these early centuries.

JAPANESE MODIFICATIONS OF FOREIGN CULTURE

It is also to be noted that the Japanese were not blind imitators. As in the nineteenth century, they were eager to take from foreign civilizations what seemed suited to their needs. They were keenly sensitive and so feared being called "barbarians" that they exerted every effort to equal in culture the most advanced peoples with whom they were acquainted. From the very first, however, they tried to adapt what they borrowed to the needs of the Japanese situation, and as time went on they more and more modified what they had received and were stimulated to make contributions of their own. They began thinking for themselves in matters of religion, and in the latter part of the eighth and the early part of the ninth century they attempted to reform the current Buddhism chiefly by developing a more nearly perfect philosophy. One form of it sought salvation, not after reincarnations through long periods of time, but here and now by a knowledge of the Buddha nature that could be acquired through wisdom.

The use of the Chinese written characters, which required a different sign for each word, was made easier by introducing signs for syllables. This reduced the total number of characters to be learned and helped to make the written language conform more nearly to everyday speech than it had in its purely Chinese dress. The Japanese syllables are in use to this day. Native schools of art and literature were developed. Even the administrative machinery was not a blind copy. The new system of administration had no sooner been completed, however, than it began to reveal a growing want of agreement with real conditions. This was partly because the Chinese models did not work well in Japan. There were three outstanding results: the control of the monarchy by the Fujiwara family through a series of regencies; the rise of a kind of feudalism; and the growth of a military class in numbers and power, ending in its control of the government.

SUPREMACY AND DECLINE OF FUJIWARA FAMILY

The Fujiwara family, next to that of the emperor the most illustrious in Japan, claims for itself divine origin. As early as the seventh century it had begun extensively to lay its hands on the government. As the strong emperors who helped in the great reorganization of the administration were succeeded by weak ones, the Fujiwara clan gradually tightened its hold in the government. It assumed but few military positions, for these were held to be socially inferior, but gradually obtained most of the important civil offices for the possession of its descendants. These held the chief governorships of the provinces and the leading positions at court. The terms of office were first lengthened, then reappointments were allowed, and eventually the various positions were held for life and transmitted to the occupants' heirs. The Fujiwara filled the government with its own members and made the offices hereditary, so that the institutions designed to weaken the power of the nobles and to strengthen the position of the monarch were used to defeat their own object. The Fujiwara, as imperial councilors, had the privilege of opening all petitions before they were handed to the throne. They saw to it that the emperors' wives were chosen from their own women, and that heirs to the throne were selected only from among sons of Fujiwara mothers. Even to-day the empress is one of the family, as have been most of her predecessors for more than a thousand years. Members of the clan were finally appointed regent and in all but name became the rulers of the kingdom. The family never, it is true, sought to steal the throne, but as the position became more sacred they saw to it that its occupant had less and less to say in matters of actual government. Finally, as soon as an emperor reached an age at which he might try to assert himself he was forced to take the vows of a Buddhist monk and retire to a monastery, to make way for a minor who could offer no opposition to Fujiwara ambitions. There frequently were several such ex-emperors living at one time.

This Fujiwara supremacy was not attained without a struggle, for from time to time the monarchs asserted themselves. Occasionally other families sought to wrest from the Fujiwara their power. The Fujiwara, however, were not to be deprived of their offices. The high posts at the court continued to be filled by them until the end of the old system in the nineteenth century. They were, however, made powerless by the introduction of a form of government by the military class. This change was brought about by a gradual evolution which was partly the result of the weakness of the system that the Fujiwara themselves had created, and partly of the growth in power of the military class.

The period of Fujiwara supremacy was one of great luxury. The court was maintained on a most expensive scale. Elaborate palaces were built and a costly standard of living was maintained. The court nobility gave themselves over to writing poetic couplets, to flower festivals, love intrigues and gambling. Many arts and pastimes were developed, partly on Chinese models, and were the basis of much of that artistic development that came to be so much admired by westerners who saw Japan late in the nineteenth century. Exquisite fabrics were produced, and fine paintings and carvings appeared. Architecture was improved: palaces and temples were built in profusion. Music was perfected. The position of dancing girls arose almost to the dignity of a profession. Festivals for viewing the flowers, for gazing at the newly fallen snow, for enjoying the moonlight, were introduced. Great sums of money were spent on Buddhist temples and monasteries and on elaborate religious exercises. Huge, costly metal images became the rage. At times half or more of the revenue of the state was spent for religious purposes. As the degeneracy of the court increased, its devotion to religious exercises was intensified. Buddhism was never more popular.

The court and its masters, the Fujiwara, were gradually losing control of the provinces and of all but the districts around the capital. Taxes to pay the expenses of the court and especially of the Buddhist church reached enormous proportions. The cost of government was increased by the necessity of administering the additional territories occupied by the expanding nation. The expenses of administration grew without a corresponding increase in the revenue, and the growing burden of taxation fell more and more upon a few of the peasantry. A system of estates free from taxation was slowly forming, resembling the feudalism of the European middle ages. By the reforms of 645 the arable land of the country was to be redivided among the people at stated intervals. For a while this plan was fairly well carried out. As time passed, however, the plan was dropped and most of the land that was reclaimed on the frontiers gradually came to be held by a few lords. As the nation grew, these reclaimed lands eventually formed the larger part of its area. Then as a reward for service or because of some special influence at court, individuals would be given estates to hand down to their descendants. Large tracts of land were similarly held by temples and monasteries as a permanent possession. Occasional laws attempted to revive the redivision of lands at stated intervals, but failed to work a lasting cure. Owners of estates frequently extended their holdings by forcibly taking over adjoining lands. These estates were partly or entirely exempt from taxation and the control of the representatives of the central government. This exemption was largely confined to temple lands and estates actually granted by the government, and was recognized by formal charters. For protection against disorder, or to escape taxation, many smaller landowners surrendered their lands to the more powerful lords and monasteries and received them back as fiefs, a custom almost exactly corresponding to the feudal system in Europe. Thus in time most of the area of the nation was made up of great, immune estates and was practically lost to the control of the government. A governor often found that only one per cent or less of the land of his provinces was subject to him. The vast majority of the landowners were bound to the central power only by a formal allegiance to the emperor. They levied their own taxes, quarreled and fought with one another, and administered a rude justice without reference to the Fujiwara-controlled court. By the end of the eleventh century the central government was ready to collapse. Robbery and military service became the only refuges from the oppressive taxation laid by the court

Nikko Temple

Torii Gate

on the lands that were not in the manors, and robbers openly infested even the streets of the capital.

FEUDAL STRUGGLE FOR CONTROL OF THE EMPIRE

During the centuries that the Fujiwara were making themselves supreme at court, warrior families were strengthening themselves in the outlying provinces and a military class was appearing. In the reforms of the seventh and eighth centuries the attempt was made to establish universal responsibility for military service, but this proved a failure. With the decline of the power of the central government, and the growth of disorder, the proprietors of the great tax-free estates were forced to depend on their followers for police purposes and for aid against their neighbors. On these estates, then, there were to be found professional soldiers who were recruited partly from the police, partly from the lords' own dependents, partly from wanderers from sections where the conditions of life had become intolerable, and partly from adventurous fellows for whom no career was open at home. These professional warriors gradually came to be controlled by a new nobility, purely military and feudal, and quite distinct from the older civil nobility that had its center at Kyoto.

This military nobility was founded by members of the imperial family who had now become nobles of inferior rank. They had sought their fortunes away from the capital, in the provinces, as local officials and as managers of the estates that were held by the absentee civil nobility. As years passed they became the actual masters of the estates they managed, or of new estates, and the leaders of the warriors who formed the only source of protection in the midst of the general disorder. The strongest of these estates were in the west, where new lands were being reclaimed, and in the north, where a long war of expulsion was being waged with the Ainu. All these estates were far removed from the corrupting luxury of the court, and by constant fighting among themselves and with the Ainu, a military class was developed, used to hardship and loyal to its leaders. The warriors, or *bushi* as they were called, became in time a hereditary caste, closed to outsiders. They possessed an ethical code all their own, the basis of the later rather elaborate *bushido* ("way of the bushi") of which we are to hear more.

With the decay of the administrative system controlled by the Fujiwara it was only a question of time until the military chiefs should struggle for the mastery of the empire. About the middle of the twelfth century the decay at Kyoto could no longer be concealed. The Buddhist monasteries and Shinto temples sheltered armed monks and desperadoes. They terrorized the weakened capital until the strong military chiefs of the provinces were called in by the distressed court to restore peace. Nothing loath, the chiefs quickly responded. The warlike monks were put down, but court intrigues and rivalries in the ranks of the Fujiwara led to civil strife which gave the chieftains further reason for interference. Finally they fell to fighting among themselves for the control of the capital and the person of the emperor. So strong was the reverence for the past and for the imperial family that no one thought of taking the throne or even the office of regent, for this last had been held traditionally by the Fujiwara. The military chiefs, however, did seek to place themselves so firmly in control that the emperor and court nobility, while retaining their ancient titles, could not hope to exert much influence on the administration.

In the long civil wars which followed, many military families sought to gain supreme control. One family, the Taira, came to power and exterminated as far as possible all who stemmed from its main rival, the Minamoto, which seemed to give promise of contesting its position. A few escaped, principal among whom were Yoshitsune, who is regarded by Japanese as their greatest military captain, and his half-brother Yoritomo, who finally gained supreme control. The exploits of the heroes of these memorable years have ever since been the delight of the storytellers of the nation and are recounted to the admiring youth of each succeeding generation.

CHAPTER IV

THE SHOGUNATE: FROM ITS FOUNDATION (1192) TO THE ACCESSION OF IYEYASU (1603)

ORGANIZATION OF THE BAKUFU

It now became the difficult task of the new military leader and dictator, Yoritomo, to organize his power so that it would remain in the hands of his family. He made peace with the powerful Buddhist monks and restored to the civil nobility lands which had been lost during the long wars. He did not attempt to take the imperial throne, nor even to remove the Fujiwara nobility from their offices. He preserved the court at Kyoto. It was still in theory the source of all power in the state, and it was encouraged to maintain its ceremonies. Yoritomo made it useless, however, by establishing side by side with the older civil officialdom a military administration loyal to himself. He appointed, in all the provinces, military constables and military tax-collectors. They did not displace the regular local officials appointed by the civil government at Kyoto, but shared and took over their authority and transacted official business with greater promptness and efficiency. Taxes were levied on all lands but those of the religious orders: the great estates of the princes were not, as during the later years of the Fujiwara, exempted from these burdens.

This military organization was called the *Bakufu*, literally "tent office." Yoritomo was its head, and in 1192 was given the title of "shogun." Strictly speaking the word "shogun," meaning "general," was not new but had for some time been a common name for military officers of the highest rank. It now took on a new significance, that of the "military dictator." The center of the *Bakufu* Yoritomo removed to the north to Kamakura, not far from the present Tokyo, where he established a separate capital. Kamakura was far from the luxury of Kyoto and from the plots of the court nobility. It was also nearer the military principalities of the north on whose support it chiefly depended.

Thus there came to be two administrative systems, the one civil, the other military, each with its own organization of officials, and each with its capital. The military, at Kamakura, of course, was the stronger, although theoretically it was under the civil. Of the elaborate organization copied from China in the seventh and eighth centuries little remained. Yoritomo must be ranked as one of the greatest political geniuses of his nation, for the dual form of government that he began lasted until past the middle of the nineteenth century, a period of more than six and a half centuries.

Yoritomo's descendants were unable long to retain the control of the machinery that he had so carefully put in operation. His house speedily suffered the fate that had befallen both the imperial and the Fujiwara families. The real power now fell into the hands of the Hojo family. The able head of that house never took over the shogunate, outwardly retaining for the position the same reverence that the Fujiwara had observed toward the institution of the emperor. The office was kept in the hands of minors, however, whose retirement was forced when they approached maturity. At first the office was reserved for the heirs of Yoritomo, but as his direct line died out, descendants of the Fujiwara or of the imperial family were appointed. The heads of the Hojo were content with the title of "regent." They wielded their power with relentless energy and controlled emperors and shoguns with an iron hand.

THE HOJO ERA (1199 TO 1333)

The Hojo era, in spite of civil strife and military rule, was not without progress in culture and art. New sects of Buddhism arose, the expression of fresh needs and of originality in religious thinking. Like the earlier divisions of Buddhism that we have mentioned, most had their origin outside Japan and were brought in from China. They were modified, however, by their Japanese adherents. One of these, Zen Buddhism, had a great influence over the military class. Enlightenment was to be obtained not primarily from books, but as Gautama had found it, through meditation. Zen demanded of its followers a type of intense mental concentration; to know truth one must learn to look at the world from an entirely new angle, and become indifferent to the hardships of life. Zen encouraged simplicity and symbolized through it the deepest meanings. It valued reserve, a perfect self-control backed by concentrated energy. Its sternness and its simplicity were in contrast to the softer teachings and ornate temples of the older sects. It impressed mightily the warrior class and while only a few practiced fully its exacting, rigorous methods, it had a great effect upon feudal life. Painting, architecture and landscape gardening, social intercourse and etiquette, literature, all showed its influence, particularly in the later feudal ages.

As time went on Kamakura, the military capital, began to take on an air of luxury and refinement. Magnificent temples were erected. Tea was introduced from China and with its use there began an elaborate ceremony of tea-drinking closely associated with the Zen sect. With tea came porcelain utensils from the continent, and in the attempt to copy them the Japanese for the first time began to produce superior pottery of their own. Sculpture flourished, especially in wood. Some specimens bear comparison with the best of the work of the Western world. Sword-makers raised their handicraft to the rank of a fine art. Two notable schools of painting developed. Once during the period Japan was seriously threatened by foreign invasion. The Mongols, a Central Asiatic people, overran Central and Western Asia and Eastern Europe, and established themselves on the throne of China. In the latter part of the thirteenth century their emperor of China, Kublai Khan, decided to attempt to take over Japan. Against the threatened invasion the Japanese united as one people, forgetting for a time their divisions. It took all their strength to repulse it. They were aided by the elements. Storms destroyed the fleets which bore the invading armies. Thus Japan remained the one civilized state in the Far East that had successfully resisted the Mongol arms.

THE ASHIKAGA PERIOD

In time the power of the Hojo was weakened. The defeat of the Mongol invasion strained their resources and the luxury of the life at Kamakura did its work. The regents became corrupt and followed the evil custom of retiring early in life, each in turn leaving his position to a child who was controlled either by his ministers or by an ex-regent. The government presented the sorry spectacle of a puppet guardian of a puppet shogun who was in turn the agent of a puppet emperor. Mismanagement followed. When dissatisfaction was at its height the emperor made a desperate effort to regain the substance of the power whose shadow he enjoyed in the form of reverence in the eyes of the masses, and to end the dual government. Years of civil war followed. Aided by one of the military families, named Ashikaga, the emperor finally prevailed. However, all was not serene and for over half a century civil war was kept up. Private feuds added to the disorder and for a time all centralized authority seemed to be doomed before a reconciliation, with the Ashikaga in power, was reached.

The two centuries (1392–1603) that followed were not destined to be peaceful. The habit of disorder had become too firmly fixed during the years of civil strife to be quickly overcome. The power of the individual military families grew, and away from the immediate vicinity of Kyoto, where the Ashikaga shoguns had located their capital, each was erecting for itself what was practically an independent domain. The powerful chiefs had their *samurai* (warriors) whose contempt for death, ruthlessness, cunning in warfare, and absolute devotion to a chief are seen in modern Japan.

Disorder extended even beyond the bounds of the empire. Daring Japanese merchant pirates harassed the shores of China, plundering and burning cities and towns, avenging the invasion of the Mongols and the failure of the Chinese to grant satisfactory trading privileges. They raided such centers as Ningpo, Shanghai, and Soochow and extended their operations to the Philippines, and to Siam, Burma, and India. For a time it seemed that the Japanese might anticipate by three hundred and fifty years their commercial development of the twentieth century.

Internal disorder was increased by Buddhist warrior-monks. Monasteries had grown rich on the gifts of pious emperors, shoguns, and nobles, and sometimes housed groups of thousands of trained fighters. In the years of disorder many of the inmates of these religious houses had armed themselves. More than frequently men assumed the robes of the priest for other than religious reasons and in time the greater monasteries had become the home of desperadoes who terrorized the surrounding country.

The anarchy (disregard of government) was still further increased by the extravagance of the Ashikaga shoguns. They had fallen victims to the luxury and vices traditionally associated with the imperial court. Their excesses had necessitated the levy of burdensome taxes. The military families, as their power grew, contributed less and less to the national treasury, and the burden of supporting the state fell on a narrowing region around Kyoto. The load finally became unbearable and the people rose in riots, refusing to pay taxes and asking that all debts be cancelled. The emperors were

About 1,500,000 Japanese are engaged in the fishing industry.

in dire distress. One Ashikaga shogun brought down on his head the curses of all future Japanese patriots by acknowledging the overlordship of China and accepting from its emperor the title of "King of Japan" in return for trading rights which added to his revenue.

The anarchy was further increased by the arrival of Europeans. The explorations of the Portuguese in the age of discoveries, during the fifteenth and early sixteenth centuries, so familiar to all students of Western history, had finally brought them to Japan. Europe had probably first heard of the country from the Venetian traveler, Marco Polo, who had spent some years at the court of Kublai Khan at the time the Mongol expeditions against Japan were being organized. He brought back to Europe marvelous tales of the riches of the islands, and it was partly the hope of rediscovering the country that led Columbus to undertake his famous search for a direct Western route to the East. It was in 1542, nearly fifty years after Vasco da Gama rounded the Cape of Good Hope, that the Portuguese reached Japan, the first Europeans to view its shores. The Spaniards, Dutch and British followed. They established commerce and brought with them two things which were to affect profoundly the future of the nation — firearms and Christianity.

Firearms were a new weapon to Japan and their use partly helped the feudal lords to become more independent of the central government. Their use also transformed the strongholds of the military chiefs. No longer were wooden structures and simple earthen walls sufficient defense. There arose great castles with massive walls of stone.

Christianity was first brought by the Jesuit, Francis Xavier, who arrived in Japan in 1549, with some Portuguese and Japanese companions. He was followed by other members of the Society of Jesus. The message of these earnest men found a quick and eager response. In ceremonial, doctrine, and organization Roman Catholic Christianity seemed to the Japanese but little different from the Buddhism to which they were already accustomed. Accepting Christianity meant a further share in the valuable trade with the merchants of the West, so they were predisposed in its favor. Buddhism had partly failed to meet the religious needs of the people and at this time was at a low ebb morally and spiritually. The new faith was favored at the capital. In less than a generation after Xavier's arrival there were reported to be two hundred churches and one hundred and fifty thousand Christians. At the height of the mission the converts are said to have numbered six hundred thousand, although this figure may be an exaggeration. Two embassies from feudal lords were sent to Rome, and for a time it seemed as though Japan were about to become a Christian country. Christianity, however, added to the existing discord in a nation with too many quarreling religious sects. What with the rivalries of the military chiefs, the Buddhist warrior-monks, the weakness of the central government, the anarchy at the capital, the introduction of firearms, and the divisions caused by Christianity, it seemed for a time that the nation might break up.

In spite of all this, there was some progress in culture. Even at Kyoto there were occasional times of quiet when the arts of peace might flourish. At the courts of some of the great feudal barons, or *daimyo* ("great name"), as they came to be called, there was to be found a regard for the refinements of life, even though the luxury of the capital was despised. Here and there were towns. The Zen sect of Buddhism and its closely allied ceremony of tea-drinking grew in popularity. Artistic dancing had its followers, and a severely classical style that was developed then remained in vogue in aristocratic circles. With the help of Buddhism the drama began its growth. The tasteful arrangement of flowers became popular as a special study. Landscape gardening received much attention. It owed its beginning, as does so much else that is good in Japan, to Chinese models, but these had been greatly improved upon. The burning of incense became very popular in polite society. Wrestling grew from its earlier and simpler forms to a specialized vocation. Sword-making, as might be expected in an age so largely military, attained the rank of a fine art. The secrets of manufacture were handed down from father to son and choice specimens were as famous as the greatest paintings and almost as costly. Painting was pursued by men whose names rank with the greatest that Japan has produced. *Bushido*, "the way of the warrior," the ethical code of the military class, was further developed.

JAPAN UNDER CONTROL OF MILITARY LEADERS

In addition, out of the anarchy of these years arose the men who were to form Japan into a strong centralized state and eliminate internal strife — vigorous leaders who made the modern Japan of today possible. Birth counted for less than it had in some previous centuries, and the man of merit and ability had a much better chance of recognition than he would have had in peaceful times. Members of the lower orders of the military class arose and struggled to establish their supremacy. Three of these stand out as successive masters of the nation — Nobunaga, Hideyoshi, and Iyeyasu. The last was to organize a form of government that was to endure until past the middle of the nineteenth century.

The first of these, Nobunaga, rose through a series of successful wars with his neighbors and made himself master of Kyoto. After serving the shogun for a while he supplanted him. From that time his life was largely a series of wars waged to maintain his position. After his death he was followed by Hideyoshi, who is one of the most remarkable men that Japan has produced, and has at times been called its Napoleon. He was of humble birth, not being even of warrior (*samurai*) rank. Iyeyasu, for a time his enemy, soon allied himself with him, and became his chief lieutenant. Hideyoshi is the one instance in the nation's history of the rise of a commoner to the highest position open to a subject.

After subjugating the nation Hideyoshi gave himself to the task of unifying and increasing his power. Not content with controlling Japan, he dreamed of foreign commercial and political expansion. Near by was Korea, and Hideyoshi planned to reduce it and use it as a gateway for the conquest of China. War was declared and carried on with a cruelty which won for the Japanese the long-lasting hatred of the Koreans. The invasion also involved the islanders with China, who claimed the peninsula as a vassal state and felt that its possession by an alien power would be a menace to her borders. The prolonged attack was only partially successful. Finally, after the death of Hideyoshi, Japanese power in the peninsula dwindled. Iyeyasu by intrigues removed the son of Hideyoshi and made himself master of the country. Slowly the quarreling feudal chiefs were crushed and the authority of the central government was reëstablished.

CHAPTER V

The Shogunate: From the Accession of Iyeyasu (1603) to the Coming of Perry (1853)

IYEYASU REORGANIZES THE SHOGUNATE

Iyeyasu now faced the great task of consolidating his conquests and insuring that they would remain in the hands of the Tokugawa. So well did Iyeyasu, and the son and grandson who succeeded him, do their work that the empire was dominated by their family for two and a half centuries and for over two centuries the country was undisturbed by war. The means that they used to achieve these ends were various. In the first place, Iyeyasu had himself appointed shogun (1603) and thus placed himself at the head of the feudalized military system that had first been organized by Yoritomo, over four hundred years before. He located the military capital at Yedo, the present Tokyo, away from the imperial court, nearer the geographical center of the main island and in the North, from which most of his support came. The city became in time the largest in the land. Its castle, the residence of the shoguns, was massive and extensive and in altered form became the modern imperial palace. Iyeyasu surrounded Yedo with fiefs (lands rented to feudal chiefs) held by members of his own family, the Tokugawa. All important points were placed in the hands of chiefs whom he could trust. Officials responsible to the shogun were put over the principal cities, and the main highway between Kyoto and Yedo was carefully guarded. Iyeyasu skillfully distributed fiefs among members of his family and loyal barons wherever

46

there seemed likely to be trouble. Thus families that might aspire to the shogunate were certain to find a strong fief organized near them or between them, and given to a Tokugawa. The funds of those barons about whose loyalty there was any doubt were kept low by enforcing them to construct great works, especially castles.

All daimyo were commanded to maintain houses in Yedo. Each was to keep some of his family or retainers there throughout half of the year as hostages for his good behavior, and each was himself to spend the other half of the year there, where he could be watched. Deputy governors under the direct control of Yedo were scattered through the country, and were still another check on the daimyo. The feudal barons were allowed a great deal of liberty within their own fiefs, and the commoners — merchants, farmers, and townspeople — were encouraged to govern their local affairs through guilds, city elders, and village chiefs. All officers were held strictly accountable for the maintenance of order, however, and a habit of discipline and obedience was acquired which was in sharp contrast to the anarchy and excessive individualism of the last years of the Ashikaga. This habit of discipline was to be of service to the nation in the great changes of the nineteenth century.

The imperial institution was not destroyed, but the emperor was barred from any active interference in national affairs by the clever trick of increasing his sanctity or holiness. His divine origin was emphasized and was held to remove him from the everyday duties of ruling and of concerning himself with the material affairs of his country. None but his closest ministers and the members of his family were to come into close contact with him. No others might see his sacred face. He was to devote himself to honoring his imperial ancestors and obtaining their blessings for the nation. He was still held, however, to be the source of all authority and the shoguns were in theory merely his servants. He was provided with a modest but sufficient income and was allowed to confer empty titles of honor. The old civil or court nobility was preserved and the sanctity in which it was held was increased, but it was provided with only small funds, and was given no part in the active administration. The appointment and term of office of the emperor's chief officials were virtually under the control of the *Bakufu*. From this same source, and not from independent estates, came the incomes of the monarch and the court aristocracy. To make sure that imperial control would not threaten, Kyoto was surrounded by many fiefs held by military lords on whose loyalty the Tokugawa could depend, and Osaka, the port to Kyoto, was governed directly by the shogun.

All classes of society were carefully controlled by minute and exact regulations. The imperial court, feudal lords, warriors, and commoners had their actions, their dress, and their food strictly standardized. Confusion and turmoil were reduced to a minimum by a most elaborate system of governmental supervision. Education, the printing of books, and especially the study and teaching of the works of the Chinese Confucian scholars were fostered, possibly in the belief that by these means public and private morality would be made stable and order become secure. The successive shoguns helped the merchant and farming classes by favorable rules and public works. This may have been done with the conviction that if the country were prosperous there would be no unrest.

CHRISTIANITY IS PERSECUTED

Iyeyasu and his successors completed the consolidation of the nation by forbidding Christianity and cutting off all but the smallest contact with the outside world. Earlier attempts to stamp out Christianity had failed to stop its spread. Foreign priests kept up their teachings and many of the inhabitants, possibly 600,000 in all, principally in Kyushu and other southern portions of the empire, became Christians. During the earlier years of his rule Iyeyasu was apparently not against Christianity and actually favored the missionaries on several occasions. He seems to have had no religious motive in this, but did it as a commercial measure. He was trying to open up and maintain trade with Europe and the lands of Eastern Asia. For a number of years commercial relations were kept up with Spain through Mexico, and the Dutch and the English were both permitted to establish trading factories in the South. Japanese merchants made their way unopposed by the shogun to the Philippines, Annam, Siam, China, and India. Iyeyasu was eager to see a merchant marine developed and Japan's mines opened. Gradually, however, his attitude underwent a change and toward the latter part of his life he opposed Christianity. His descendants were even more bitter and ended not only by driving out Christianity underground but by closing the country against all but the slightest contact with the outside world.

It is difficult to ascertain all the reasons for this policy, but a few are apparent. An envoy sent to Europe reported unfavorably on what he had seen of the foreign religion in its own home. A shipwrecked Englishman painted in an unfavorable light the history of the Catholic Church, encouraging the suspicion that the teachings of Spanish and Portuguese missionaries were but the preliminary to political aggression. A Christian plot was discovered against the shogun and his authority was defied by a Franciscan father. There were many quarrels and rivalries between the different missionary orders. The missionaries, especially the Jesuits, obeyed their religious superiors rather than the civil authorities, an attitude that the shoguns, who were trying to insure internal stability by centralizing all power in their own hands, did not like. The Spaniards tried to shut out the Dutch, and the Dutch in turn tried to shut out the English from the Japanese trade.

In 1614 Iyeyasu ordered that all foreign priests be expelled, that all churches be destroyed, and that all Japanese Christians be compelled to give up their faith. His determination to stamp out Christianity was reënforced by the persistent refusal of the missionaries to leave Japan. They hid themselves, or were deported only to return. Such a disregard for authority was bad for the peace and unity that it was Iyeyasu's chief ambition to establish. Iyeyasu died (1616) before he could fully carry out his policy of repression. His descendants, however, continued and made more severe his anti-Christian policy. Missionaries persisted in coming to Japan and many of the native Christians refused to renounce their faith. Their stubborn disobedience strengthened the fears of the shoguns. It seemed evident that the prestige and possibly the supremacy of the Tokugawa family was at stake. To the alarmed Yedo chiefs it was even conceivable that Japanese independence might be threatened.

Christianity was barred primarily on political, not on religious grounds. As in the early Roman empire, Christianity seemed to mean treason. The most severe measures were adopted to stamp out the Church. Missionaries and converts were apprehended by the thousand and on refusing to renounce their faith were killed, many of them by the most cruel methods. The fine heroism of these martyrs but heightened the apprehensions and determination of the Tokugawa officials. The persecution of the Christians ended in a rebellion in 1638 when most of the remaining Christians rose as a unit and made a last stand in an old castle not far from Nagasaki. They were wiped out by the government troops and the church practically ceased to exist. The rules against it were strictly enforced until well into the nine:eenth century. Registration in the Buddhist temples of all persons was made compulsory. All Japanese were forced to show allegiance to some branch of Buddhism, and all suspected of not being loyal were required on pain of death to tread on the emblems of the Christian faith. Only in one or two remote localities, and under disguised forms, did Christianity persist.

FURTHER ISOLATION — JAPAN CLOSES HER DOORS

The stubborn resistance of the Christians aroused in the shoguns a suspicion of all foreign trade. For a time the effort was made to keep up the much desired commerce with the Spaniards and Portuguese, but as the persecution of the Christians became more severe and missionaries continued to come on their nations' vessels, the Yedo officials decided that all trade with Spain and Portugal must be stopped. When, in 1640, the Portuguese tried to resume trading, their messengers were beheaded. To make certain that no disturbing influences would invade the empire, all Japanese were forbidden to leave the country and any one who succeeded in doing so was to be executed on his return. The building of any vessels large enough for over-seas traffic was forbidden. The English had for a few years maintained their trading factory but found it unprofitable and closed it. They later desired to reopen commerce but were not permitted to do so.

Of all European nations only the Dutch were allowed to continue to send ships. They were more interested in the profits to be made from trade than in the spread of their Protestant faith. They had even helped the Tokugawa officials to get rid of the Japanese Christians. Less fear therefore was felt of them. Still, they were Christians,

and to the frightened officials at Yedo were not entirely
above suspicion. Their trade drained the country of money
and restriction was gradually increased until they were
eventually allowed to come only to one port, Nagasaki.

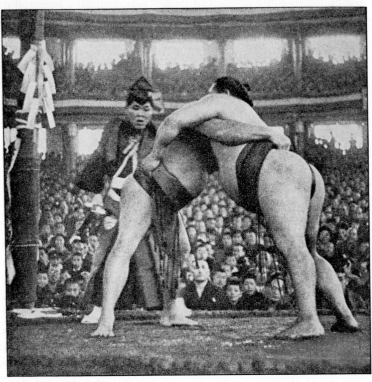

Sumo, Japanese wrestling, is of very ancient origin and still a favorite sport.

There their merchants were carefully confined to a small
island and were forbidden to hold any religious service.
Only a few ships a year could come and the number was
eventually reduced to one. Only once a year could any of
the Dutch come ashore, and then merely to make a strictly
guarded journey to Yedo to pay their respects to the shogun.

The most minute regulations were adopted for all dealings with them. In spite of the humiliations the Dutch continued their trade because for many years it was highly lucrative. They brought in silk and piece goods and these they exchanged for gold and copper which sold in Europe at a large profit.

With this slight exception, Japan was now tightly sealed against influence from the Western world. The land entered on more than two centuries of hermit life. A few ideas filtered in through the Dutch, and a carefully regulated onesided commerce was carried on by the Chinese who, at this time, were themselves almost equally well sealed against contact with Europe.

EFFECTS OF THIS ISOLATION

The Tokugawa organization had at last insured internal and external peace. The centuries of disorder and civil strife had come to an end. The system, however, carried within it the seeds of its own destruction. Warlike in its origin and purpose, an organized military feudalism, all its strength was now directed to stopping warfare and promoting internal order. Its decay was inevitable The years of peace led to great changes within the nation. For the first time since the seventh century Japan began to be a unit. The Tokugawa system forced it to cease to be a group of warring clans, and to act as a whole. True, the forms of feudalism were preserved and the fiefs still existed. National unity was not complete, but the barriers that had helped to divide the nation were being weakened. Although the *Bakufu* issued no extensive codes, it published a system of rules by which the actions of every subject were carefully ordered. Obedience to laws issued by a central authority was becoming a habit.

Moreover, the nation was becoming more prosperous. With order insured, the farmer and the skilled worker could pursue their occupations without fear. The state encouraged agriculture and undertook irrigation works. Peasant proprietorship of land increased, and village self-government was strengthened. Roads were improved. Internal commerce grew. The attention of the military chiefs was turned from fighting to the pastimes of peace. Luxury sprang up, and extravagant amusements, methods of dress, eating, and living became common. The wishes of the mighty were catered to by a merchant class which itself became wealthy. Commercial capital was built up and the currency was improved. Although there were occasional famines and epidemics of disease, population increased. There was but little poverty, and the cities had no slums to compare with those of the Western world.

Education became fairly widespread and literature and art flourished. In the capital and the homes of the daimyo, schools were established and the sons of the rude soldiers became scholars. Lecture halls were maintained for the common people. There was much study of the Chinese classical writers. For the first time in the nation's history the avowed followers of Confucius became numerous. There had been for many centuries a few in nearly every generation who called themselves such, but the teachings of the Chinese sage had never previously been accorded so wide a hearing. There were many lecturers on Confucianism, and different sects arose. Most of the upper classes became Confucianists, and while still supposedly following Buddhism, rather openly regarded the Indian faith as a mass of superstitions and fit only for the unlettered masses.

The state encouraged the collection of books. Historians became popular and made extensive studies of the nation's past. Painting and ceramics (clay pottery work) reached new heights of achievement. Colored prints of everyday things and a popular literature were developed to please those of the lower ranks. Famous works of architecture were being produced. The old Japan was perfecting its culture. The old warrior or samurai class was decaying. It is true that its ethical code, *Bushido*, was being elaborated more

Kendo, the art of fencing with bamboo staves

than ever before into a formal system and that martial exercises and ideals were encouraged. However, the spectacle of a military caste being served by the entire nation and yet having not fought for decades, was inconsistent. Luxury was sapping the strength of the feudal soldiers. The heirs of the great daimyo were falling under the control of their retainers, much as the emperors in the old days had fallen under the control of the Fujiwara and then of the shoguns. Even the shoguns were at times dominated by their ministers.

Moreover, the increased leisure for study and its encouragement by the *Bakufu* had turned men's thoughts to the past. Japan's history was delved into and compiled and with the work came a renewed love of things Japanese. The language was studied and organized. A Japanese literature, as opposed to one in the classical Chinese, was developed. Shinto, the old native cult, was revived, and with its revival came an increased reverence for the emperor, its head. Buddhism, although it had been made a state religion by the Tokugawa in their efforts to stamp out Christianity, was looked at askance by these patriots, for it too was a foreign faith. But more important politically was the discovery by the historians that the emperor was the rightful ruler of the nation and that the shogunate was a comparatively new idea. Among a group of scholars the conviction gained ground that the shogun must resign and that the emperor must be restored to his rightful place as the actual as well as the nominal head of the nation.

Reënforcing the renewed emphasis upon the institution of the emperor, was the interest in Chinese classical literature. The Tokugawa officials, when they promoted its study, could not have appreciated how subversive the writings of the Confucian school could prove to the *Bakufu*. The Chinese classics emphasized the position of the monarch and knew nothing of the dual system that existed in Japan. Loyalty to such ideals could not but weaken the position of the shogun, for according to them he was but a minister of the emperor and had stolen the power of his master.

The great feudal estates of the South, former rivals of the Tokugawa, and never completely contented with their rule, could be counted on to aid in any attempted restoration of

Judo, the art of self-defense, Japanese style

the emperor, if for no other reason than that it might give
them an opportunity to place a new family on the seat of
the shogun. So indirectly the power that brought about
the study of literature was threatened by it.

Japanese archery is an elaborate ceremony as well as a form of recreation.

IMPENDING CHANGE IN NINETEENTH CENTURY

By the middle of the nineteenth century the nation was ripe for change. The old order was decaying. The vigor of the Tokugawa shoguns had so declined that they were more and more controlled by their ministers. Rumors of dissatisfaction and unrest were beginning to be heard. Some revolution was seemingly about to take place. What form it would have taken had there been no interruptions from without, it is hard to say. By one of the strange coincidences of history, however, just as the old Japan was about to pass it came into contact with the expanding Western world and out of this contact a new nation emerged.

CHAPTER VI

THE CIVILIZATION OF THE OLD JAPAN

One cannot well begin the story of the change from the old to the new Japan without stopping to describe the main characteristics of the nation's culture just before the beginning of the change. Modern Japan is so decidedly the child of the Japan of 1850 that to know the child one must be acquainted with the parent.

THE MILITARY CLASS

One of the prominent features of the culture of Japan in the nineteenth century was the strong position of the military class. This military class, usually headed by the shogun or his ministers, had from the time of Yoritomo controlled the state. The few emperors who attempted to assert themselves were forced to rely as firmly upon an army as did the shoguns. There had been gradually built up a system closely resembling the feudalism of medieval Europe and like it primarily military in its forms and ideals. Its name, *Bakufu*, and the title of its head, *shogun*, were martial. Underneath the shogun were the great military lords, the *daimyo*. Associated with the daimyo were minor chiefs and especially the samurai, the ordinary knights or soldiers. Their position was hereditary and as a sign of their rank they proudly wore two swords. Most of the *samurai* owed allegiance to some baron or to the shogun. From their lords they received a stated allowance. Only a few, called *ronin*, "wave men," were unattached. Their freedom was not normal and was due either to an unusually adventurous spirit, or to some calamity, such as poverty, disgrace, sorrow, or the extinction of their liege's house. The warrior classes had developed their own code of ethics, *Bushido*. The lower social orders seemed to exist for the support of this fighting caste. A wide gulf divided the samurai from the commercial and agricultural classes, and the young bloods of the lower orders paid the warriors the sincere flattery of an imitation in dress and manners carried as far as the laws would allow. The ideals of the nation, as is usually the case, were molded by the standards and the exploits of the military class.

The presence of this military class was in many respects to be a distinct advantage to Japan in the new age brought by contact with the West. It provided a group of disciplined men accustomed to leadership, and whom the nation had been trained to follow. With a few exceptions the leaders in the transition from the old to the new Japan were of the military class. Until 1945 the government was dominated by their successors. Japan, under the leadership of her samurai, and especially under the influence of her martial tradition, found it comparatively easy to adjust herself to European ways. She proved an apt pupil in learning the modern methods of warfare. The obedience, physical courage, and willingness to fight bred by the ages of her military past had a very large part in enabling her to make herself feared by Western powers and to assume a place among them. Japan, as we shall see, felt compelled to assume the defense of the entire Far East against the West. For her eagerness to attempt this Japan must partly thank the training given by the years of military feudalism.

The warrior class was organized by fiefs. The feudal system produced loyalty to the local lord rather than to the state or the emperor or even to the shogun. The shogun as head of the Tokugawa family had his personal retainers and his vassals who were true to him, but the land had many daimyo who were jealous of his power, and the samurai who owed them allegiance could be counted on to obey their lord first, and the shogun second or not at all. Although much weakened, and thoroughly subordinated to loyalty to the emperor, this feudal spirit persisted in the later Japan.

THE IMPERIAL INSTITUTION

Another powerful survival from Japan's earlier days is the institution of the emperor. The ruling house was devoutly believed to have reigned from ages eternal and to be the direct offspring of the gods. It formed the rallying point for the ardent spirit of patriotism which has been so marked a characteristic of the recent Japan. The emperor's sanctity had been emphasized, thus strengthening his hold on the imagination of his people and heightening the new-born patriotism of the nineteenth century. Moreover, the precedent had been maintained that he should reign but not govern, and the change to a constitutional monarchy of the European type was an easy one. From the shogun who exercised absolute authority in the name of a holy sovereign who but seldom interfered in the administration, to a ministry, likewise acting for the monarch, was no difficult step. Under both, the emperor has been the source of all authority but has exercised little of it himself. This does not mean that in the new age there has been a ministry responsible to a parliament, although toward this goal there now seems to be marked progress. It does mean that a group of the ablest in the land won the ear of the emperor and governed in his name, assuming all responsibility for his acts. Just how much personal influence the emperor exerted has never fully been known.

MODERN OUTGROWTHS OF OLD IDEALS

The *patriotism* of the new Japan, the self-conscious nationalism which so centers in the institution of the emperor, has grown up largely in the past seventy years. Strange as it may seem to those who know only the Japan of the twentieth century, there was but little of what we think of as patriotism until nearly the close of feudal days. The intense national spirit of today is, however, partially an outgrowth of features of the older Japan, the loyalty of the samurai to his lord, a keen sensitiveness to ridicule and insult, the solid foundation produced by the Tokugawa shoguns, and the atmosphere of sanctity that surrounded the emperor. The individual samurai, as we have seen, had originally little if any feeling of attachment to the emperor at Kyoto or to the nation. He would probably not have tolerated the taking of the throne by one not descended from Jimmu Tenno, and the samurai resented the invasion of the land by the Mongols, but it was not until well along in the Tokugawa régime that even some of his class began to be passionately conscious that the country was the "land of the gods" and to be sensitive to the lack of power of the rightful sovereign. The samurai did, however, have a real sense of loyalty to his lord. Part of his code of ethics was to be willing to sacrifice all that he held dear, wife, children, life itself, in the service of his master. At the latter's death he might even commit suicide. So extensive indeed did self-destruction become on such occasions that it was necessary for the early Tokugawa shoguns to seek to restrain it by law. The spirit of personal loyalty was during the old régime directed toward the lord, but with the passing of feudalism it centered itself on the person and institution of the emperor with an intensity which it is hard for foreigners to appreciate, and contact with the nations of the West wakened into life a hidden but earnest love of country.

Another characteristic of the code of the samurai was extreme *sensitiveness on points of honor*. Personal insults were often avenged by death. Emphasis was laid on the Confucian idea that a son must not live under the same heaven with the murderer of his father and the stories of the vengeance of sons upon the assassins of their parents are numerous. The servant pursued unto death the slayer of his lord, even at the cost of his own life and that of his wife and children. The sword of the samurai was ever ready to be drawn to maintain what he deemed his honor. He was intensely proud of his rank, at times boastfully so. This pride seems almost to be a racial characteristic, for it is older than feudalism. It has survived the latter, and it is national as well as personal. It helps to explain the resentment of the Japanese at the discrimination against their fellow-countrymen in the Western world. They strongly resented the attempts at exclusion by law from the United States and Canada, partly, it is true, because of the economic disadvantage at which they were placed, but primarily because these measures, which applied to no Europeans, seemed to brand them as inferior and so to be a slur on their national honor.

Another characteristic of both the old and the modern Japan was *bureaucracy* — the predominance of state supervision and social, as contrasted with individual, initiative and activity. As we have seen, all phases of life were subject to regulation and supervision by the shogun's representatives. Foreign commerce was under official control. Order and peace were maintained by the most rigid conformity to law. Collective responsibility was enforced; the family was held accountable for the deeds of its members, and the village for those of its inhabitants. Partly as a result, in the new Japan social action has been emphasized to a high degree. The state has taken the lead in encouraging railways, telegraphs, banking, and foreign commerce. The Japanese merchant

marine, for example, whose growth was lately so noteworthy, received much government aid. This emphasis upon
collective action had many advantages for Japan in the twentieth century, when the nations of the West were tending to
decrease state direction of industry, transportation, and commerce.

The agency by which state direction has been exercised
under the later régime has been the bureaucracy. This has
been one of the outstanding features of the administrative
system of the recent Japan. Its higher positions have been
filled largely from the ranks of the samurai and their descendants. It has formed a ruling body that has on the
whole dominated the nation. It is a continuation in another
form of the spirit of the Tokugawa, a careful and minute
control by the government of all phases of human activity.

Another characteristic of the old Japan was its experience
in *assimilating foreign culture*. The civilization of the pre-
feudal ages, as we have seen, was developed largely through
contact with China. Even during the feudal ages, so dis-
tinctly Japanese, the country was at times and in some phases
of its life much affected by the continent. Japanese standards of action, while largely the outgrowth of the people's
social needs, were partly molded by Confucian and Buddhist
ideals. Bushido, while unmistakably Japanese, showed the
effect of both Confucianism and Buddhism. Family life
and solidarity bore the imprint of continental influence.
Feudalism grew up partly as the result of the failure of the
attempt to adapt the administrative system of China to
Japanese conditions. The written characters of China were
taken over bodily and its literature was read as eagerly in
Japan as on the continent. Buddhism, so influential in the
old Japan, was Indian in origin and reached the islands in
Chinese garb. Chinese philosophy profoundly influenced
Japanese thinkers.

And yet the people of Nippon were not blind imitators. As much as they admired the civilization of the continent, they were not content to be slavish copyists. Bushido is very different from Confucianism and Buddhism. The Chinese written language was partly adjusted to Japanese needs by the invention of syllabic marks. A true Japanese literature and art were produced, as different from continental models as was any national art or literature in medieval Europe from those of the Roman world. The Japanese were not overwhelmed by the flood of culture from the continent. Instead they built on it a civilization of their own.

This experience in assimilating alien ideas and institutions was an admirable preparation for the coming of the European. Japan had for centuries been accustomed to take and adapt new ideas from abroad. Her national pride caused her to be fearful of any charge of barbarism, and her past made it natural for this pride to lead her, not to reject the culture of the Western world but to hasten to adopt as much of it as she needed. She had assimilated the civilization of the Chinese, the highest that she had known. Once she was convinced that that of the West was more powerful she was quick to seize upon it for herself.

Nor is it strange that Japan, having been so apt a pupil, should think herself a competent teacher. Now that she had so successfully learned of the Western world she posed as the instructor of the other and less expert peoples of the Far East. To her schools came students from all the Far East.

THE CULTURE OF OLD JAPAN

Still another characteristic of the old Japan was its esthetic sense. This artistic sensitivity has shown itself in painting, sculpture, ceramics, lacquer, and architecture, in landscape-gardening, in an elaborate code of politeness, in flower festivals, in the tea ceremony, in the manufacture and decoration of swords, in dancing, and many other ways. It would be out of place in a book of this size and scope to go into any but the briefest of discussions of these, interesting as they are. Art was largely influenced by Chinese models. There were developed, however, vigorous native schools, and even in following the foreign schools the Japanese showed originality. Like the Chinese, Japanese works

Horino

Characters and characters: in spite of the difficulties of the written language, literacy is widespread.

of art show the strong influence of Buddhism. Like them, too, the ideal is not so much a photographic reproduction of nature, as an attempt to catch its spirit, to portray emotions as much as matter. Painting has a long and brilliant history. The collections to be found in America and Europe and the enthusiasm of its Western students bear witness to its appeal to a more than national artistic sense. Illustrations for books and wood-engravings were begun as a means of education and amusement for the common people. There was color printing of broadsides and illustrated books also primarily for the masses. This seems to have been distinctively a Japanese idea and not to have been introduced from the continent.

There were noted sculptors in wood, and workers in metal, including those who erected the great bronze statues of Buddha. Lacquer and inlay work were known and remarkably well executed. Porcelain had long been imported from China before it was produced in Japan, but the Japanese later spent much labor and skill in its production. The best examples of the architecture of the past are to be found in Buddhist temples and in the few remaining feudal castles. The well-known buildings that adorn the tomb of Iyeyasu at Nikko, for example, are the delight of all who have seen them. Part of the landscape gardening is too strange to appeal to us, but most of it has real charm. Some of it is in miniature, and stunted trees are trained with great care to reproduce the forms of those of normal size. The flower festivals at the cherry blossom season are national holidays.

The leisure of the imperial court circles and later of the daimyo under the Tokugawa gave opportunity for the people to express themselves in elaborate and exquisitely perfect etiquette. Japanese politeness became proverbial. The ceremony of tea drinking with its different schools and exact regulations, the development of the burning and judging of incense into an elaborately ordered pastime of the leisured, the skill that went into the manufacture and decoration of the sword of the samurai, all seem to be outgrowths of a spirit that sets great store upon the beautiful. Dancing, much of it ceremonial, goes back to the earliest historic times and is said to have taken its rise in the days of the Sun Goddess. The esthetic spirit has of recent years been at times used for commercial purposes, but it still survives and is one of the characteristics of Japan.

Of the *literature* of the old Japan but little need be said. Here, although rather less than in the fine arts, she was strongly influenced by China. In poetry as well as in prose she largely conformed to foreign models. This poetry, because of its peculiar rules, defies translation into Western tongues. Japan has had the drama, said in its beginning to have been associated with Shinto, but later deeply colored by Buddhist ideas. Still later it became non-religious and popular in form and content.

Japan has not shown a creative spirit in *philosophy, ethics,* or *religion* equal to that which molded the life of China, India, or the Semitic races. The Japanese have rather been content to adapt differing foreign systems to their own needs, and to build on contributions from abroad. The philosophers of China were studied and at times criticized. Buddhist priests arose who thought with a sufficiently vigorous independence to be founders of new sects, but no Japanese has appeared who ranks in originality with the great philosophers.

Family solidarity is one of the characteristics of the old Japan that have persisted in spite of the altered conditions of a new age. It has been one of the ever present factors in Japanese life. Each man must be loyal to his parents, serving them while they are living, honoring them after their death. The family must be continued by male heirs that the forefathers may not lack descendants to pay them honor. Marriage was common to all and, lacking offspring, adoption could be resorted to to continue the ancestral line. Obedience to parents has been one of the chief virtues. The family was more important by far than the individual and each must adapt his wishes to it. The individualism of the Western world would have been unheard of. Here the influence of Chinese teachings and models has been very great.

The wife was more obedient to the husband than in China. Absolute obedience, self-effacement, and fidelity were required of her, and yet her husband might be unfaithful or divorce her almost at will. Within her sphere she might be greatly honored, but she was always the subject of her lord.

By Ewing Galloway, N.Y.

The unit in Japanese social life is the family.

It must be added, however, that the Japanese wives were not without their charm, and a very real one. Those of the higher classes were models of simple courtesy; they had a decided influence over the younger years of the children, and left a strong stamp, chiefly for good, upon the morals of each new generation. The work of the women of the feudal classes, while unspectacular, was noble and far-reaching in its effects. The wife by her intense loyalty and self-effacement inspired her husband to maintain his ideals and to preserve toward his lord something of the same attitude. The wives of the lower classes of society were real helpmates for their husbands and frequently shared in the breadwinning. There have been empresses on the imperial throne, although only two of these have sat there in recent centuries.

RELIGION AND ETHICS OF OLD JAPAN

In religion the Japanese have not been creators of the first rank. They have been religious, and deeply so. Their fine loyalty has made them willing to die for a faith once adopted, as was seen in the persecutions of Christianity. But their religious sentiments seem to be influenced largely by their appreciation of the beautiful and by a matter-of-fact attitude toward life. They have not been given to original philosophical or religious ideas nor even to changes in the field of ethics. They have largely been liberal in choosing their religious beliefs and these are either foreign in their origin or have been profoundly influenced by foreign ideas. Their primitive faith, it will be remembered, seems to have been a very simple affair. They honored various spirits, the many divinities that had been created by the childlike attempts of the race to account for the beginnings of the world, of life, and the nation. There were the Sun Goddess and hosts of other deities. The spirits of great warriors were revered. There were no images, no elaborate temples, and no priestly caste. Such ethical standards as existed had little connection with religious belief.

Under the influence of continental thought and institutions, this primitive religion became much changed. The primitive faith seems to have been modified to build up the power of the monarch and to emphasize his divine origin. For centuries the native cult was, as it still is, primarily associated with the ruling house.

Philip Gendreau, N.Y.
A Shinto holy man in his ceremonial robes

Buddhism came in, and for the first time the native faith achieved self-consciousness and was given a name, *Shinto*, Chinese in origin, meaning "the way of the gods," as distinguished from *Buppo* "the law of the Buddha." For a time Shinto seemed about to be absorbed by Buddhism, for clever monks identified the Japanese divinities as incarnations of Buddhist saints and deities. *Shinto* persisted, however, in the imperial household and in shrines through the country. During Tokugawa times it was revived by the group of scholars who were seeking to emphasize the native as contrasted with the foreign, and the attempt was made to purify it of many of its alien elements. It passed over from the Tokugawa to the new age and with the restoration of the emperor achieved a marked official extension in a more purely native form. Its temples are now, as they have traditionally been, simple buildings, reproducing more nearly than any other structures the form of the early Japanese house. They have caretakers, who form a sort of ruling body of priests but are not powerful as a class. There is no image within them, but there are emblems of the god, usually a sword, mirror, or jewel, the insignia said to have been given by the Sun Goddess to the imperial ancestors. Before the shrines are the *torii*, resembling ornamental gateways. There was and is no ethical system enforced by Shinto, and it makes for but little sense of moral or spiritual guilt. Its ceremonies are confined to purification, to honoring the spirits of emperors, of national heroes and ancestors, to entreating blessings on the nation, and asking for protection from evil.

In *Buddhism*, on the other hand, the old Japan had a most highly developed religion. The faith had come to the nation with all the wealth of the philosophy, art, and organization that it had acquired in the course of its growth in India, Central Asia, and China. Its philosophy was elaborate, teaching that this world is but a passing show, a delusion; that man is chained to it and to suffering in an endless series of rebirths, his lot in each new one being determined by his *karma*, a term that is rather lamely but succinctly defined as meaning the sum of his actions good and bad in preceding existences. Man is to seek and to find salvation by escaping from the changing world and the chain of existence through the means provided by the faith. These means, it may be recalled, were various, differing somewhat with each sect. Buddhism had a tremendous literature. It erected magnificent temples, adorned with all the beauty and skill known to the art of the lands through which it had passed, and with the gifts of generations of pious believers. Its unmarried priesthood formed a powerful body, often noted for learning, devotion, and ability. It had been the principal vehicle by which civilization had been brought to Japan, and it had received the support of generations of emperors, nobles, and feudal chiefs. Buddhism, indeed, occupied in Japan much the position that the Catholic Church held in the Europe of the middle ages. Both were the means of bringing to a semi-barbarous people a superior and older civilization. Both dominated society by their philosophy, learning, and priesthood, and their elaborate rituals, their art and architecture. In the later years of the Tokugawa, it will be remembered, Buddhism began to lose its hold on the thinking men of the nation. The masses still believed in it, but the educated were inclined to follow the teachings of the great philosophers of the Confucian school. It must not be thought, however, that there was the sharp division between religions that one finds in the West. The Japanese for some purposes would frequent the Shinto shrines, for others the Buddhist temples, and could still pay reverence at his ancestral graves and follow the moral teachings of the Chinese sages without any feeling of inconsistency. Even if he had largely lost his faith in Buddhism, he would still resort to its burial rites for his kinsmen.

Confucianism has been a determining factor in the life and thought of Japan. From the time that continental culture had first reached the islands the Chinese classical writings had been studied, although by only a few until the Tokugawa régime. Beginning with Iyeyasu, Confucius was honored and Chinese literature and the Chinese sages were extremely popular with the military class. Even after the Japanese revival of the middle and later years of the Tokugawa, when the native religion, language, literature, and institutions were given renewed attention by many scholars, Chinese ethics remained popular with most of the samurai. The effects of Confucianism on Japan were many. Ancestor worship flourished. Loyalty of the vassal to his lord, complete obedience of children to the will of their parents, subordination of the wife to the husband even to the point of self-effacement, were encouraged. The moral precepts taught in the schools today are largely Confucian in their form.

Bushido, the ethical code of the military class, reminds one of the chivalry of feudal Europe. It was the result of years of development. It seems to go back at least to the time when the military class was forming. Under the successors of Iyeyasu it was elaborated and largely made over until it lost some rather unlovely features of its earlier years. It was essentially Japanese, but in its later and elaborated form it showed the influence of Confucianism and Buddhism, especially the former. Loyalty was the cardinal virtue of bushido. The samurai must sacrifice life, truth, and even his family if the service of his lord required it. With the passing of feudalism the nation, personified in the emperor, has absorbed the loyalty previously paid to the daimyo. The devotion to one's parents and ancestors, although subordinate to loyalty, was prominent. Family unity, promoted by this devotion and by the duties of brothers to one another, was marked. Economy, simplicity of life, and indifference to wealth were exalted. For recreation military amusements were encouraged. Bread-winning pursuits and regard for money affairs were held in contempt. The warrior above all valued self-control in the presence of pain, and steeled himself to endure the most intense agony without flinching. Personal honor was highly valued and the sword of the samurai, the sign of his rank, although it must not be drawn but for the gravest reasons, was ever held ready to avenge a slight to its owner or to its owner's lord. Honor was dearer than life and in many cases self-destruction was regarded not simply as right, but as the only right course. Disgrace and defeat were atoned for by suicide, and on the death of a daimyo loyal followers might show their grief and affection by it. The knight might protest against grave injustice by suicide, and might by the same means try to stop his lord from unwise or unworthy action. Part of the training of every samurai was the ritual for disembowelment, *hara-kiri*, the approved means of self-destruction, and one of the highest tests of his character was to be able, if the occasion demanded, to perform it calmly and without flinching. If condemned to death, it was held to be a privilege to execute the sentence on one's own body and to be a disgrace to die at the hands of the public headsman. This repression of emotions and disregard for the material accessories of life were especially encouraged by the Zen sect. This, it will be remembered, had been marked by a stern discipline and fostered self-reliance, and had been modified by Confucianism.

The wife of the samurai was also influenced by bushido. She was to be self-effacing, and was to hide all traces of suffering or grief. She was taught how to end her life simply in case the occasion seemed to demand it. By her example she exercised a profound influence over her husband.

It must not be thought that bushido, any more than chivalry, was lived up to by all those who professed to be guided by it. The samurai seldom attained to even his own standards.

As in the case of chivalry, bushido profoundly influenced not only the upper classes, for whom it was primarily intended, but the civil population as well. The lower orders of society copied as far as possible the ethics as well as the manners of the warrior. Bushido, like chivalry, was to remain an active force long after the social order that had produced it had disappeared.

Such were the more prominent features of the organization and life of the old Japan. They were to be greatly modified and some of them later disappeared, but they have left an unmistakable stamp upon the ideals and the culture of the nation.

CHAPTER VII

The Period of Internal Transformation (1853–1894)

I. FROM THE COMING OF THE FOREIGNER TO THE RESTORATION OF THE EMPEROR (1853–1867)

In a preceding chapter we have seen how the Tokugawa régime gradually prepared the way for its own destruction and the end of feudalism. By the middle of the nineteenth century the time was ripe for a change. The successors of Iyeyasu had become feeble and were largely controlled by their ministers. The more influential rivals of the Tokugawa were disloyal. The great fiefs of the southwest, especially Satsuma and Choshu, far removed from Yedo, were practically self-governing in all local affairs and would not stand for the interference of the shogun's officials. As a result of the long peace, luxury and idleness were working havoc with the warrior class; military feudalism was fast becoming outdated.

A Japanese revival, which so far was largely confined to a relatively limited circle of scholars, was emphasizing the historic position of the emperor and was spreading the conviction that the shogun was an unauthorized ruler. The court nobles at Kyoto were beginning to be restless under the control of the *Bakufu*. The middle classes, increasingly prosperous, could no longer be regarded as existing merely to support an idle, outdated warrior caste. Some sort of change was bound to come. Whether, if there had been no outside factors, the nation would simply have been plunged into long civil war from which one of the feudal families would have emerged in possession of the shogunate, or whether the constitution of the state would have been entirely altered, it is hard to say. As it was, the revolution was hastened and its course determined by the coming of the foreigners.

THE OCCIDENTAL ADVANCE IN THE NINETEENTH CENTURY

The seclusion to which the Tokugawa had confined Japan was remarkably effective, but its success was not due entirely to their efforts. During the latter part of the seventeenth and all of the eighteenth century Western nations did not try too hard to force their way into either China or Japan. In China only one port, Canton, was open to foreign trade. The Portuguese had ceased to be an important factor in the Far East. The Spaniards were content to occupy the Philippines and did not reach out for more commerce. Great Britain was busy extending her possessions in India and in making them secure against the natives and the French. All European nations were busy at home with the great wars of the seventeenth, eighteenth, and early nineteenth centuries. By the middle of the nineteenth century, however, a change was taking place.

In the latter part of the eighteenth and in the early nineteenth century, Russians, English, and Americans had explored the North Pacific. The peace that followed the Napoleonic Wars was making possible a more nearly undivided attention to commerce and manufactures. The Industrial Revolution was stimulating trade. Markets were being sought for the enormous quantities of goods produced by the new machinery. Fresh sources of raw material were necessary to supply the demands of the enlarging factories. Steam navigation and the railway were making it possible to reach the ends of the earth in an unprecedentedly short time and to transport goods in quantities hitherto undreamed of. In North America the expansion of the United States had brought European peoples to the east coast of the Pacific; Oregon and California were settled in the eighteen forties and fifties. The Russians had reached the west coast after a mighty advance across the vast reaches of Siberia, and had formed settlements in the Amur country and Alaska. Before long the Pacific would teem with a new commerce and the nations of eastern Asia would be compelled to open their doors. By 1850 nearly all India had been brought under either the direct or the indirect control of Great Britain. The English, having found China's restrictions on trade intolerable, had fought a war with her which was ended in 1842 by a treaty opening five ports to trade and making provision for commerce and official intercourse between the two nations. This treaty was quickly followed by others between China and the leading powers of the Occident. It was inevitable that pressure would soon be put on Japan to end her hermit existence.

During the first half of the nineteenth century there were repeated indications of an approaching attempt of Western powers to open Japan. The Dutch, through their closely regulated intercourse at Nagasaki, brought news of impending changes. Here and there Japanese were learning Dutch and through the medium of that language were getting an inkling of the importance of the civilization of Europe. A few European works on history, geography, literature, and science were read. From the time when some native surgeons dissected a human body and found that it was more accurately described by the Dutch writers on anatomy than by the Chinese, there were those who saw that the culture of the West was in some respects superior to that of the East, and wished to know more of it. Russian ships appeared on the northern coasts as early as the eighteenth century, and envoys from the Czar asked (1804) that regular trade be established, only to be met with an outright refusal. Russians and Japanese came into conflict in the Kurile Islands and Sakhalin, and the Japanese were beaten. The Russians might have forced themselves on Japan proper had the Napoleonic Wars not intervened to take their attention elsewhere. In 1846 a French ship touched at the Ryukyu Islands and advised the islanders to place themselves under French protection as a guard against the British. In 1847 the king of Holland advised the Japanese to abandon their policy of exclusion, and in 1849 warned them that an American fleet might soon be expected. Ships of other European nations touched at Japan from time to time.

THE PERRY EXPEDITION AND RESULTS

Fortunately for Japan the move that opened the country was made by the United States, a power that had no territorial ambitions in the Far East. The American merchant marine was at that time relatively much more important than it became after the War Between the States. American ships had gone to all corners of the earth and in the Far East were second in numbers only to those of England. Japanese fishermen occasionally wandered across the Pacific to the Aleutians or to the coast of North America. In 1837 one ship, the *Morrison*, made its way nearly to Yedo in the effort to return a few such castaways, and, if possible, to open commerce. She was fired upon, and returned to Canton without having landed her charges. American whaling vessels gradually became numerous in the North Pacific and in several instances were wrecked on the Japanese islands. The surviving sailors were confined, often handled roughly, and as a rule were returned to the outside world only through the kindness of the Dutch. Some arrangements were necessary with the shogun's government to insure good treatment and rescue for the crews. In 1846 an American commodore asked in the name of the president that trade be opened, only to be refused. In 1848 the American brig *Preble* threatened to bombard Nagasaki unless fifteen foreign seamen held there were immediately handed over.

California was acquired in the forties, and ships were soon sailing from San Francisco to the new treaty ports of China. Since Japan lay in the direct path of such vessels, its ports, if opened, would offer convenient places for restocking with water and provisions, and for refitting. The shipping, especially the whaling interests in the United States, asked the government to insist that the country unlock its doors. Finally the American government responded and sent a squadron under Commodore Perry to obtain a treaty. In 1853 Perry arrived in Uraga Bay near Yedo with a fine display of force, transmitted the president's letter to the Japanese authorities, and since there seemed to be no immediate prospects of successful negotiations, sailed away, announcing that it was his intention to return the following spring. His coming created a great commotion in Japan. The shogun's ministers were greatly perplexed. Even the imperial court was stirred and ordered prayers said at the great national shrines. Perry returned, according to promise, the following spring. Before his steam warships the Yedo authorities felt themselves powerless, and after some negotiations concluded a treaty.

Japan's isolation was not yet entirely at an end. The Perry treaty did not provide for the complete opening of the country. Its emphasis was not upon commerce, but upon the care and safe delivery of shipwrecked sailors, and the provisioning and refitting of passing vessels. Two ports were opened, one (Shimoda) near Yedo and one (Hakodate) on the northern island. An American consulate was to be permitted at Shimoda; trade was to be carried on only in accordance with local regulations, which might be severe;

supplies for vessels were to be purchased only through Japanese officials. The *most-favored-nation clause,* customary in the West, guaranteed to Americans any concessions that might be made to other powers. In the two years following the Perry treaty similar treaties were obtained by England, Russia, and Holland, but in none of them was residence or extensive commerce and trade provided for.

Spencer Byard

Commodore Perry took along this miniature railroad train (from an old print) when he made his second trip to Japan in 1854.

In 1857 Townsend Harris, the United States consul-general, obtained for American citizens the privilege of residing in the open ports, to which was now added Nagasaki. *Extraterritorial* rights were assumed by the foreigners. This meant that the latter were under the rule of their consuls and not of Japanese officials and laws. Commerce was provided for in 1858 by a further treaty with the United States, also brought about by Harris, which remained for many years a model document of its kind and was in force until 1899. By this last treaty customs duties were provided for, and a fixed scale was agreed upon which was not to be changed without the consent of both nations. The reception of diplomatic representatives at the court and the opening of an additional port were also granted. It ought to be added that Townsend Harris obtained these treaties from the shogun, not by any display of force, but mainly by his sympathy, tact, and persistence.

The provisions for extraterritoriality and the treaty-established tariff were a partial sacrifice by Japan of her rights as a nation, the struggle to regain which was to be a prominent feature in Japan's history for forty years. By the first foreigners were removed from the control of Japanese courts: by the second the nation surrendered the right to establish its own tariff dues. Both were very unpleasant to the sensitive, patriotic spirit of the people after their importance was recognized. Almost at the same time as the American treaty of 1858 similar ones were signed with Great Britain, France, and Russia, and others soon followed with twelve more Western powers. Just at this time France and England were engaged in a war with China, in an attempt to force her doors still further open. As an added effort at European expansion in the Far East this war probably had some influence in hastening the negotiations of the new Japanese treaties. To ratify the American treaty Japanese envoys were sent to the United States, the first diplomatic mission to visit foreign lands.

DIFFERING VIEWS ON ADMISSION OF FOREIGNERS

The negotiation of these treaties was not supported by all of the Japanese. In fact, the coming of the foreigner divided the nation into three camps. The fighting between these three groups was, within a few years, to bring to an end the dual form of government, and to pave the way for a change in the political structure of Japan. One camp was made up of those who recognized the superiority of Western culture, and the impossibility of ignoring it. They were in favor of receiving the foreigner, and learning from him as quickly as possible in an attempt to match him with his own weapons and at his own game. As Japan had in years past adopted Chinese civilization, the highest that she then knew, so these reformers would have the nation now accept that of the West, for it was proving itself to be more powerful and efficient than that of China. This group, at first very small, was to predominate within a decade and a half. As time went on it saw that the dual form of government was old-fashioned and a handicap in dealing with the centralized powers of the West. Some of its members began to work for the restoration to the emperor of the powers exercised by the *Bakufu*. In this respect they found themselves in agreement with the native school of historians who had come to regard the shogun as an illegal ruler. A second group saw the impossibility of remaining a hermit nation, but believed in opening the door only as far as was insisted on by the powers. That was the prevailing sentiment at the court of the shogun. The third believed in keeping the door tightly shut, in breaking all agreements with the Westerner, and in ousting him and all his ways. This opinion was for much of the time the prevailing one at Kyoto.

The imperial court was not in contact with the foreigner and the holder of the throne was supposed to be in favor of the third camp. The court was, moreover, from time to time under the control of the Western fiefs. Of these the most prominent were Satsuma and Choshu. From the time of Iyeyasu they had paid the shogun only a grudging submission; thus they were not inclined to yield him unquestioning obedience in his decision to admit the foreigners.

At first they had no fixed ideas on the question and were divided both between and among themselves. In time, however, they arrived at the conviction that to admit the Westerner was treason and that they should oppose it with all their might. They sought to win the ear of the emperor and induce him to assert his authority and compel the shogun to cancel the treaties.

THE SHOGUN'S DIFFICULT POSITION

The struggle increasingly centered around Kyoto. Each faction hoped that the emperor would side with them. Part of the time the Western fiefs had his ear, and inspired by them he ordered the shogun to expel the barbarians. The shogun could not comply, for he knew himself to be powerless before the cannon of the foreign gunboats. Nor did he dare to refuse point-blank, for that would be acclaimed by his opponents as disobedience to his master, and the rising tide of national sentiment would not allow such an insult to the legal head of the state. The shogun therefore delayed his decision. On the one hand he promised Kyoto to carry out its wishes but asked for leeway. On the other he continued his contact with the powers but delayed as much as possible the granting of concessions, so much so, in fact, that foreigners, not understanding his problem, accused him of insincerity.

THE END OF THE SHOGUNATE

The situation was fast becoming an impossible one for the shogun. The numbers of Westerners in the treaty ports were increasing. Commerce was growing. Even Christian missionaries were entering and, sheltered by the foreign settlements, were spreading their faith in spite of the anti-Christian sentiment bred by two hundred and fifty years of edicts to prohibit Christianity. Serious clashes occurred between the reactionary feudal lords and the Westerners. Foreigners were frequently attacked and occasionally killed by samurai who thought thus to show their anger against the barbarian who had violated the sacred soil of Japan, and to aid in his expulsion. In 1862 some Englishmen chanced to meet the followers of the daimyo of Satsuma on a public road and violated, ignorantly, the Japanese etiquette for such occasions. They were attacked by the lord's followers and one of them was killed. The Yedo government made ample apology and paid an indemnity, but the Satsuma baron refused to surrender the guilty samurai as the English demanded and the shogun was not strong enough to compel him to do so. The British therefore in 1863 sent a naval force to the Satsuma dominions in Kyushu and bombarded the capital (Kagoshima).

The other leading Western fief, Choshu, determined in the same year to take action against the hated barbarians. It commanded the straits of Shimonoseki, the narrow passage through which passed foreign ships on their way between Shanghai and the east coast of Japan and North America. An edict from the emperor had been issued without the knowledge of the shogun, ordering that the foreigners be expelled. Choshu gladly obeyed, and the forts at the straits fired at several vessels, American, Dutch, and French. The powers concerned, together with Great Britain, joined in demanding of the shogun that the ferocious daimyo be punished, but this the *Bakufu* was quite unable to do. In fact, the Choshu lord killed the ambassador sent to him from Yedo.

The four powers now sent a squadron to Shimonoseki, bombarded and demolished the forts, and destroyed the daimyo's ships. That feudal lord thereupon promised the powers that he would not rebuild his forts nor bother foreign ships and also agreed to pay the sum of three million dollars. The shogun sent an expedition against Choshu to punish the fief for not obeying his orders, but could accomplish nothing. He paid the indemnity when Choshu failed to do so. The last installment of the indemnity, it may be added, was not paid until 1875. The Americans' share proved much larger than was necessary to cover the costs and damages sustained, and later they returned a large portion of it to the Japanese.

The foreign ministers had at first been ignorant of the true nature of the relation of the shogun to the emperor. They had regarded the shogun as the supreme ruler of the land and the emperor as a kind of high priest. In the course of time they discovered their mistake and after the Shimonoseki affair the able British Minister, Sir Harry Parkes, led in a demand, which had been planned before his arrival, for the renewal of the treaties by the emperor. Backed by an allied fleet, the request was presented not at Yedo, but at Hiogo, a port near Kyoto. The immediate opening to foreign residence of that city and Osaka, the port of the capital, and a reduction of the customs duties were requested. Terrified by the show of force, the emperor issued an edict assenting to the treaties, and the promised reduction of the tariff was agreed to. This incident finally made apparent the failure of the shogun. He had not closed the land against the foreigner as he had promised: he had not even been able to prevent the barbarian from threatening with his fleet the entrance to the imperial city. He had been treated by the foreigners as a minister who was fast losing his power with his master. The emperor, under the guidance of the Western fiefs, vigorously asserted his authority and disgraced the *Bakufu* for the bungling way in which its representatives had handled the negotiations at Hiogo. The shogun resigned, but the emperor was not yet ready to assume the responsibility of accepting his resignation.

The young shogun soon died and was succeeded by a mature man who attempted to restore the waning fortunes of the Tokugawa by a cordial acceptance of Western methods. He began the reform of his army and navy and of the Yedo court, and continued to try to bring the Choshu fief to obedience. He was too late, however, to save his office. An increasingly strong national sentiment demanded that the weak Tokugawa return its power to the emperor, and in 1867 the shogun recognized that to attempt longer to keep up the dual government would be to bring disaster on himself and on the nation. Accordingly he resigned (October 14, 1867), and an imperial decree followed declaring his office abolished and the dual government at an end. Some of the followers of the Tokugawa resented the manner in which Kyoto, under the control of the Western fiefs, was accomplishing the transfer of the government from the *Bakufu* to the emperor, and revolted. They were quickly put down by the loyal daimyo, however, and the prestige of the imperial power was now even greater than before. The system first founded by Yoritomo, seven centuries before, had been brought to an end, and the emperor once more exercised direct control over his domains.

CHAPTER VIII

THE PERIOD OF INTERNAL TRANSFORMATION (1853–1894)

2. THE REORGANIZATION OF THE GOVERNMENT FROM THE RESTORATION OF THE EMPEROR TO THE WAR WITH CHINA (1868–1894)

The end of the shogunate marks the beginning of a new age. Henceforth the official policy of the nation was reform on Western lines. The leaders who brought about the emperor's restoration had come to recognize that the foreigner must be accepted. At their advice the monarch announced his intention to stand by the treaties with the Western nations made by the shogun, and to supervise directly the relations with the powers. Only eight months before the resignation of the last shogun had come the death of the emperor Komei. Although only a young man, he had been loyal to the old order, and in so far as his own personal opinions went was rabidly anti-foreign. His successor, Meiji (Meiji is the name given to his reign. His personal name, by which he is frequently referred to in foreign books, was Mutsuhito.), was a lad of only fourteen when he took the throne, and was naturally under the influence of his advisers. As he attained manhood he heartily accepted the ideals of the new age. Although the progress of his reign was due primarily to his councillors, he did not hinder them by reactionary tendencies. He was hardworking, tactful, and sanely progressive. He had the good judgment so to accept advice and so to act in conjunction with his ministers that it is hard at times to determine just how much positive

Brown Brothers

The Meiji Emperor — Japan's first modern emperor

influence he had on the policies of his reign. Had he been more domineering and less tactful and well poised, he might have been a serious hindrance instead of a help, and his reign would have had a different history. By ill-advised acts he might have come to grief.

The Western fiefs that had been so instrumental in bringing about the downfall of the shogun had at first done so because of hatred of the foreigner. As time passed, however, they became convinced that the Westerner could not be expelled. Satsuma and Choshu, two of the leading forces in the coalition, had experienced a change of heart after their rough handling by the foreign fleets. They realized that the "barbarian" was in Japan to stay, however much they might dislike him, and that he could be met only with his own weapons. They became hearty champions of Western methods and provided modern equipment for their troops. Each family may possibly have hoped to substitute itself for the Tokugawa in a kind of revised shogunate, but as time passed they saw that the old order could not be revived and that the control of the government must be exercised through other channels. Their followers together with those of two other Southern fiefs, Hizen (in Kyushu) and Tosa (in Shikoku), dominated the new government, although not quite so completely as the Tokugawa had the old, and were to maintain that mastery for many years. The army and navy were under their control for a long time and their voice was very strong in national councils. But the shogunate was dead and national affairs were henceforth to be conducted through the instruments of the new age, a bureaucracy, the cabinet, and the Elder Statesmen.

THE CENTRALIZATION OF THE ADMINISTRATION

To the support of the young emperor came all the radicals, a growing number, who desired a complete reorganization of the nation, and who saw in the restored imperial authority the opportunity to develop a monarchy and a government of the European type. The revolution of 1867 had been the work of these men, most of them samurai of the lower ranks, not nobles, and they were to be the real builders of the new

Japan. The old order was not to die without a struggle; all the nation had not yet heartily accepted the foreigner. From now on, however, the history of the country was to be one of steady development and transformation. The "year period" that nearly spanned the emperor's reign was called Meiji, "enlightened government." (The Japanese have the custom, derived from China, of dating events not by centuries or by reigns, but by reign names. The Meiji era began January 25, 1868, and ended with Mutsuhito's death, July 30, 1912.)

From 1868 to 1894, when foreign affairs began to be dominant in the national mind, the chief interest of the nation was to be in domestic reorganization. The main features of this period may be conveniently classified under political and constitutional development, foreign relations, economic progress, intellectual, educational, and literary changes and religious and ethical changes. The constitutional and political changes can best be treated first.

The end of the shogunate was of course only the first step toward the reorganization of the government. The first need of the state was centralization. The nation must act as a unit if it was to succeed in competing with Occidental powers. It must have a political machine that would operate on every individual in the land, and that could be directed by a united executive. The first step toward centralization had been taken when the shogunate was abolished, but it was only the first step. There was no adequate machinery for carrying on the government under the new régime, because for nearly eight hundred years the emperor had delegated his authority to the *Bakufu*. At first (1868) a kind of ministry or council was formed, intended to be somewhat like the one copied from China. It was made up of members of the Western fiefs and of the court nobility. It could be but little more than a makeshift, pending the time when something better could be found. In it provision was made for a gathering of the samurai and court nobility. This assembly, which actually met in 1869, was an unsuccessful attempt to adapt to Japanese use the representative governments of the Occident.

In 1868 the capital was moved from Kyoto to Yedo, which was now renamed Tokyo, "Eastern Capital," and the emperor took up his residence in the castle-palace of the shogun. The change emphasized the break with the seclusion and lack of power of the past, and the assumption by the emperor of the functions formerly intrusted to the shogun. No longer was the monarch kept in veiled seclusion, but rode out openly to show his face to his subjects and to receive their worship. The transfer of the capital also brought the emperor nearer to the geographic center of his lands, and by establishing the seat of his government on the coast it gave an unmistakable demonstration of his frank and cordial acceptance of intercourse with foreigners and eased his relations with them. This attitude toward the Westerners was reënforced by an edict denouncing all violence against them, and by an imperial audience to the representatives of the treaty powers.

Shortly after the restoration the emperor's advisers put in his mouth a "charter oath" to indicate the lines on which future changes were to be made. This remarkable document has been somewhat freely translated as follows:

"The practice of argument and debate shall be universally adopted and all measures shall be decided by impartial discussion.

"High and low shall be of one mind, and social order shall thereby be perfectly maintained. It is necessary that the civil and military powers be concentrated in a single whole, that the rights of all classes be assured and the national mind be completely satisfied.

"The uncivilized customs of former times shall be broken through, and the impartiality and justice displayed in the working of nature shall be adopted as a basis of action.

"Intellect and learning shall be sought for throughout the world, in order to establish the foundations of the Empire."

Here was a combination of the old and the new, a mixture of Chinese and Japanese thought and wordage with Western ideas. The philosophy of Confucius, the foreshadowing of parliamentary government, the centralization of the state, the determination to learn from the entire world, were all in it.

With the oath came another adjustment of the machinery of government, including principally a council of state which was to have the control of the government for some years.

With the passing of the shogunate and the coming of the new age, feudalism was evidently out-dated. Already under the peace imposed by the Tokugawa it had begun to lose its strength. Its armies, in which the individual prowess of the warrior and the glory of each fief were valued more than discipline and group strategy, would be of little use in defense against a European power. Its decentralization was a handicap in the struggle for national solidity and reorganization. With the loss of its head, the shogun, and the reassertion of the authority of the civil arm, represented by the emperor, its continuation would be abnormal.

The reform leaders, as a rule drawn from the ranks of the samurai of the more progressive fiefs, were the first to recognize the wisdom of abandoning the old system, and a public clamor for abolishing feudalism began. Civil officials were appointed to represent the central government in each of the fiefs, and a bureaucracy controlled by Tokyo was thus begun. In 1869 the four great daimyo of the Southwest offered to the emperor the registers of their lands and people as a symbol of the transfer to him of the local administration.

Then followed a remarkable spectacle, a splendid example of the old loyalty and the newly aroused patriotism of the empire; the vast majority of the nearly three hundred remaining feudal lords voluntarily surrendered their fiefs. No longer was the allegiance of the samurai to be first of all for the daimyo; no longer was Japan to be a loose collection of fiefs. The love of country, prepared by the centuries of union under the Tokugawa and the loyalty developed by Bushido, was newly aroused by contact with Western peoples. This love of country made possible a unified administration under the emperor. The daimyo were not, however, moved purely by patriotism to surrender their fiefs. Strong pressure was brought to bear on them by the reformers. Numbers of them had long exercised little authority: in the decay of feudalism the real power in many fiefs had fallen into the hands of ministers and retainers, and the daimyo were not averse to giving up a power of which they had only the shadow. Moreover, the central government guaranteed the feudal estates incomes of one-tenth of their former revenues, and the expenses of local administration need no longer be met by them. The surrender of the fiefs was followed (1871) by an imperial edict which finally abolished feudalism.

The pensions which were promised the ex-daimyo and samurai proved to be so heavy a drain on the national treasury that before many months the emperor's advisers were endeavoring to find some means of reducing them. In 1873 a plan was announced for exchanging the pensions for cash and government bonds. Although the established proportion for the exchange provided the samurai with sums the return from which would be much less than their pensions, many of them willingly accepted, partly out of patriotism, partly out of ignorance of business methods, and partly because the code of the samurai had insisted that it was beneath his dignity to be seriously concerned about money. Before long (1876) exchange was made compulsory and the special support by the state of an hereditary warrior caste came to an end.

The end of feudalism was followed in the course of the next few years by acts which perfected as thoroughly a centralized government as the most highly organized states of the West. In the first place, for the old feudal army made up of contingents furnished by individual fiefs and recruited exclusively from the samurai, there was substituted a national army, drawn from all ranks of society. To no class was there now reserved the privilege of defending the state; the opportunity for doing so was not only offered, but forced upon all by a system of compulsory military training and service which applied to men of suitable age regardless of station or birth. The new army was first patterned after French models, and then, following the Franco-Prussian war, after the German system.

An act closely related to this nationalizing of military service was the removal of many of the old social distinctions. The difference between the civil or court nobility and the military class was abolished. The new aristocracy that was later created was neither civil nor military, but national. The former distinctions between the warriors and the commoners were cancelled. Within the commoner class itself the ancient gradations which had condemned certain groups to hereditary dishonor and had imposed on one of them the scornful title of "not human" (hi-nin) were annulled. Many of the samurai voluntarily laid aside their swords, the badge of their rank: in 1876 the rest were compelled to do so. All subjects of the emperor were now on an equal footing in the eyes of the law. From the ranks of the ex-samurai, however, came most of the leaders of the new Japan, and while the class ceased to have a legal existence, individual members of it, by force of character and tradition, were to dominate and guide the nation for years to come.

In place of the local administration by feudal lords, an elaborate bureaucracy was organized. Its members were appointed by and were responsible to the authorities in Tokyo, and to it was intrusted the entire administration of the country, local as well as national. Through it the humblest subject of the emperor was protected and supervised by the direct representatives of the monarch himself. At its beginning the bureaucracy was naturally recruited largely from members of the samurai class, for these were the only ones who were trained in governmental administration. No one was allowed to hold office in the fief of which he had been a member, however, and as time went on the ranks of the civil service were recruited from the successful candidates at competitive examinations. These last were open to all classes, regardless of birth, and helped to bring into official life large numbers of men who were not of the military class. The model for this bureaucracy was found partly in the reforms of the seventh and eighth centuries. The Japanese, however, were influenced as well by Western models, the example of Germany being especially strong later.

The leaders in the reform movement early planned a national code of laws. The feudal customs of the old days, varying from fief to fief, could not meet the conditions of the new age. Moreover, extraterritoriality, which seemed to reflect on the character of Japanese courts and laws by exempting foreigners from their jurisdiction, was extremely distasteful to the sensitive Japanese. Urged on by the hope of ending extraterritoriality by removing the cause for its existence, the new government pushed as rapidly as possible the formation of codes along Western lines. By 1871 two volumes of the criminal code were ready and some offenses against foreigners were tried by it. The use of torture and of punishments which, judged by Western standards, are excessive or barbarous, was abolished. Trial by jury was not adopted, but a judicial system was begun and every effort was made to make it efficient and above reproach.

The currency system was thoroughly reorganized and nationalized. Under the old régime many kinds of money had been in circulation, both coin and paper. Paper money suggested by the Chinese practice had been in use, and each fief had felt itself free to issue it. The result was confusion and instability. The newly centralized government was under the necessity of starting a uniform national currency. The support of the mercantile classes would thus be assured, and every new coin and bill would be evidence to the public of the power of the emperor and the Tokyo administration. National prosperity would also be promoted. A commissioner was sent to the United States to study its finances. On his return the decimal system was introduced, a new coinage was issued, and a plan of national banks and paper currency was adopted which resembled the one in use in America.

At the time of Perry the ratio of gold to silver in Japan had been about four to one. Foreigners had quickly taken advantage of the situation and had bought up all of the gold that they could lay hands on, exporting it under the protection of the treaties. As a result the distressed Japanese officials altered the ratio to the fifteen and then the sixteen to one then in use in the West. But in the meantime gold had disappeared and the cheaper silver had taken its place. The process was helped by an unfavorable balance of trade. The bimetallism of the nation was destroyed by these agencies and the currency was reduced practically to a silver basis; the nation was not to go on a gold basis until after the Chino-Japanese war. Before many years a financial crisis made necessary a reorganization of the banking

system and the American plan was modified by the foundation of a central national bank along the lines so common
in Europe. This strengthened the control exercised by the
central government over the banking organization of the
nation, and aided as well in the marketing of the government
bonds and in the financing of its other undertakings.

An official revival of Shinto was encouraged to increase
the respect paid to the emperor. Under the early Tokugawa,
Buddhism had had more official favor shown it than had
Shinto, possibly because of the aid it gave in the effort to
expel Roman Catholic Christianity from the islands. During
the last years of the Tokugawa a Shinto revival had helped
to pave the way for the restoration of the emperor's power.
After 1869 Buddhism, while still recognized, was discouraged
and Shinto became the official cult of the nation. Shinto
was made to emphasize more than ever the memory and
achievements of the emperor's ancestors, and became closely
identified with the growing spirit of patriotism. Through
Shinto a religious tinge was given to the love of country.
Patriotic and religious enthusiasm combined to emphasize
national consciousness and unity.

A national postal service was begun even before the end
of feudalism, and, supplemented by a telegraph system introduced and managed by the government, it became an efficient instrument for promoting national consciousness. The
new national school system, of which more will be said later,
was directed from Tokyo and also helped to strengthen the
unity of the country.

The agents of this transformation and centralization were
a group of young, able men, drawn almost exclusively from
the ranks of the samurai. For the most part they were those
who had early seen the necessity of admitting the foreigner
and adjusting the nation to his ways, and who had made
themselves familiar with Western civilization either by resi-

Prince Yamagata, first to forge an empire

dence abroad or by diligent study and travel. Prominent among them were Iwakura and Sanjo, court nobles; Kido, Yamagata, Ito, and Inouye, all four of them samurai of Choshu; Okubo and Saigo, both samurai of Satsuma, and two other samurai, Itagaki and Okuma, the one of Tosa the other of Hizen. Others equally famous in their time might be mentioned, but these names at least should be remembered by all who seek to be familiar with the new Japan. Most of them were from the South and Southwest, from those fiefs which had been prominent in bringing about the restoration. Under them the control exercised by the southern feudal estates over the government was to be maintained for many years. These men had the ear of the emperor and dominated the civil bureaucracy and the army and navy.

OPPOSITION TO THE NEW ORDER

The centralization of the government, although relatively and strikingly rapid, was not the work of one year or of two, and was not finished until the middle of the eighteen eighties. But it was not completed without a struggle with the forces of the old régime. The mass of the nation, it is true, was increasingly in sympathy with the reform leaders, but nearly every step in advance met with violent opposition. It was some years before Westerners were entirely safe from the swords of anti-foreign rowdies and fanatics, even though the emperor had placed the strangers under his special protection. These anti-foreigners haunted the unlighted streets and alleys of Tokyo at night and attacked unwary foreigners. The emperor's ministers were often in personal peril of violence from these agitators, and at least one, Okubo, actually lost his life at their hands. Not all the nation could see that the changes were wise. Many bitterly resented the abandonment of time-honored Japanese customs and methods for the foreign ways. Revolts broke out from time to time, only to be put down.

In 1877, the opposition started a well organized rebellion in the South, the suppression of which taxed the powers of the new government. The leader of the rebellion was Saigo, a samurai of Satsuma. He had been among the reformers in the earlier stages of the reorganization movement. However, he had broken with the majority of the group who were at the head in Tokyo. He had wished to preserve military service as the exclusive privilege of the samurai, and had opposed the creation of the national army recruited by conscription from all ranks. He had, moreover, favored a war with Korea. That country had broken off relations with Japan when the latter admitted the foreigner, and Saigo would have avenged the insult with an armed expedition. Since war would check internal reorganization, the more radical reformers opposed him and Saigo retired from the cabinet. Leaving Tokyo, he went south to Satsuma and there began gathering around him all the forces of discontent. Imposing in person, able, a fine example of the traditions of the samurai of the old school, he soon found himself surrounded by a strong army. All those opposed to the acts of the ministry, to the seeming abandonment of the nation's individuality, flocked to him. He was supported by the ex-daimyo of Satsuma, who was himself of the moderate conservatives.

In 1877, the Satsuma malcontents raised the standard of revolt against the government. Saigo allowed himself to be dragged into the rebellion as its head. Against them were brought the forces of the new national army in which commoners and ex-samurai fought side by side. The Tokyo government called out more troops than were actually needed, partly to demonstrate to the nation the efficiency of the new system and partly to insure victory. The fighting was fierce, but the outcome was not long, if ever, in doubt. The Satsuma rebels were defeated and those of their leaders who escaped death in battle committed suicide. The new order had met the old on the field of battle and had conclusively demonstrated its superiority. The new national army, drawn from all classes, had overwhelmed the forces of feudalism and serious armed opposition to the new age was at an end.

THE MOVEMENT TOWARD CONSTITUTIONAL GOVERNMENT

The triumph of centralization was but one phase of the political transformation of Japan. No less important was a movement toward constitutional government, the result of contact with the democracy of the West. All thorough-going reformers were united in demanding the end of feudalism and the restoration of the emperor. One group of them, however, was in favor of an absolute government (autocracy) supported by a bureaucracy, and another believed that the elected representatives of the nation should have an important share in the government. The one found in Germany and the Prussian system a model which more nearly than any other in the West represented its ideal. It was supported by the conservative ex-samurai and retained control of the government. The other group represented different shades of opinion, but in the main saw its ideal in England and the limited monarchies of the West. It advocated placing the administration in the hands of a ministry responsible to a parliament elected by the nation.

Constitutional government was seemingly foreshadowed in the charter oath of 1869 when the advisers of the young emperor put into his mouth the promise that "argument and debate shall be adopted and all measures shall be decided by impartial discussion." The exact meaning of this promise was and is a matter of some dispute. Some held it to be a definite promise of parliamentary government; others maintained that it did not have any Western institution in mind. The latter position is probably more nearly correct. The framers of the oath seem to have intended nothing more than an assembly of the feudal states and the court nobility, for with the exception of the loss of the shogun feudalism was still largely intact at the time the oath was taken. The samurai and nobles would meet by virtue of their hereditary positions, not as elected spokesmen of the nation. Such an assembly did convene in 1869. Its functions were to ascertain the opinion of the warrior and noble classes, the only groups which had in the past been concerned with the active government. The gathering proved a failure. Membership in it was not highly esteemed, and it accomplished nothing of note. The government was carried on through other agencies. In 1873 the gathering was dissolved.

Although the institution which seems to have been contemplated by the charter oath had failed, the oath itself was to be taken up by the liberals and to be interpreted as a promise of a truly national assembly with extensive powers. By 1873 the statesmen of the nation knew more of Western institutions than they had in 1869. An official mission had visited America and Europe and had been much impressed by what it had seen. On its return to Japan one of its leaders (Kido) presented to his colleagues in the government a memorandum advocating a constitutional monarchy, but did not suggest any very definite institutions through which this should be carried on. This was the true beginning of the struggle for representative government. The history of subsequent developments is an interesting one, but only its main features can here be presented. The movement drew its support principally from two groups of people. The first was made up of the radical wing of those who favored the adoption of Western ways. They advocated an enthusiastic and wholesale Westernization of Japan and were in favor of discarding all the customs and institutions which from the foreigners' standpoint marked the nation as peculiar and barbarous. They wished Japan to take its place at once with Western powers by copying all the trappings of Western civilization. The younger students, both those who were returning from America and Europe and those who were the product of the new schools in Japan, some of the editors of recently established newspapers, and some of those who were in intimate contact with foreign books or foreigners in the treaty ports, formed the bulk of this group. The more extreme among them had taken or were to use many of the most radical political theories of the West. They were to read the books that had preceded the French Revolution, such as Rousseau's *Social Contract*. No one ever talked of abolishing the monarchy: the imperial institution had too firm a hold on the imagination of the nation for that. Many did, however, believe in a ministry responsible for all its acts to a national assembly elected on the basis of a voting population. The second group was made up of some of those of the governing class who had broken with the men in power, and who desired to make political capital out of the agitation. They apparently hoped that by championing the constitutional movement they would either oust the ministry or force it to make terms with them.

Early in 1874 a group of officials who had differed from the government on its Korean policy and had resigned, presented a memorial protesting against the arbitrary acts of the heads of the bureaucracy and advocating an elective assembly. The government was inclined to make concessions to these former officials, apparently in the hope that it could win their support and forestall more demands later. Accordingly a compromise was arranged by which the two factions were reconciled and important constitutional changes were agreed upon which were a step, although a very short one, toward representative government. A senate was established as a legislative chamber. It was to have deliberative powers but not those of initiating measures, and it was to be made up exclusively of appointed members of the noble and official classes. There was to be a reorganization of the departments, including the establishment of a high court of justice, to obtain a separation between the judicial, executive, and legislative branches of the government. This was obviously done under the influence of the theory of the division of functions that so greatly influenced the constitutions of the West. In addition, an assembly of the governors of the prefectures was to be convened to bring the Tokyo authorities in touch with the needs of the people. None of these changes provided for popular election or for representation of any but the official classes, but they were meant to limit the absolute power of the group that surrounded the emperor. The nation was probably not ready safely to take advantage of further concessions.

The changes promised in 1874 could not, however, be expected permanently to satisfy the liberals. Neither the senate nor the assembly of governors proved very effective, and of course, since they were representative only of officialdom, both were easily controlled by the ministry. By 1877 the agitation for a constitution was again in evidence. It was more insistent than before and was no longer confined to liberal or dissatisfied members of the ruling class. Radical ideas were spreading under continued contact with the democracy of the West, and political bodies sprang up which advocated representative institutions and sent out lecturers and agitators to instruct and arouse the people. The movement grew in intensity, and in 1878, moved by the assassination of one of the prominent ministers, the government partially gave way and announced the organization of local assemblies. These were elective bodies, chosen by a limited franchise. There was to be one in each prefecture and they were to be merely advisory to the governors. They were to meet for one month each year and were to have a voice principally in the levying and spending of local taxes and in the supervision of accounts. They could also petition the central government. On the whole these assemblies worked well. Later (1880) similar ones were organized in the cities, towns, and villages. Occasionally they came into collision with the representatives of the central government, but they served to give the people a voice in local finances and were training schools for the national parliament.

The grant of these local assemblies did not, however, silence the liberals. Their demands were only increased as no national assembly was yet provided for, and revolutionary ideas from the West were spreading with each month that intercourse with Westerners continued. Memorials asking for a national assembly were presented to the government by various bodies. A convention of the liberal clubs met, and by a demonstration emphasized their desires. Many of the newly founded newspapers championed the movement. Finally, in October, 1881, the government yielded and in the name of the emperor promised that a national assembly would be convened in 1890 and that a constitution would be granted. The next year Ito was sent abroad to study the form of constitutions in use in the West, and became on his return the head of the commission that was to frame a similar document for Japan.

Of Ito it ought to be added that he was the most prominent statesman of Japan in the last two decades of the nineteenth century. He had begun life as a samurai of Choshu and was originally, like his master, anti-foreign. He early

Prince Ito, advocate of Western progress Keystone View Co.

became convinced of the necessity of reform after Western models, however, and together with Inouye and three others, in 1863, braving the edicts which still made it a capital offense to go abroad, secretly went to Shanghai. From there he and his companions sailed to London, Ito and Inouye working their passage before the mast. In London the latter two spent a year, studying. When Choshu became embroiled with the powers, Ito hurried back to Japan in an attempt to prevent his fief from persisting in its attitude towards foreigners. He did not succeed, and for a time was in peril of his life. After the restoration, however, and the frank recognition by the country of the new age, he quickly rose in office, and was for years to be a dominant figure at Tokyo.

FORMATION OF PARTIES, PARTY AGITATION

Following the promise of 1881 for a national assembly, three parties arose to prepare the way for government under a constitution, and to mold by their action the terms of that document. The first of these, called the Liberal Party, had as its leader Itagaki, who had earlier been a member of the group that had helped guide the nation through the Restoration. He was a strong advocate of giving the people a voice in the government and his party represented the extreme wing of the radicals. He has sometimes been called the Rousseau of Japan, and while the parallel is not an accurate one, he and his party stood for what they deemed the rights of man. Occasionally the more rabid members of his party employed violent measures to further their cause.

The next party was the Liberal Conservatives. Its leader was Okuma, another ex-samurai. He had early acquired a knowledge of English and Dutch and with it a conviction of the need of reforming Japan. He had been a member of the government and had remained in it longer than had

Itagaki. Having chafed under the strong control exercised over the administration by the ex-samurai of Satsuma and Choshu, he finally broke away and organized a party, apparently in the hope of weakening the Sat-Cho (Satsuma-Choshu) combination by bringing into the government the element of popular representation. The Liberal Conservatives were the more moderate wing of the advocates of representative government. They favored a gradual extension of the franchise, the development of local self-government, and a policy of internal reorganization as opposed to imperialism. They stood also for a sound currency. The party would naturally attract to itself many elements in the nation which, while opposed to the Sat-Cho control, were not willing to go to the lengths proposed by Itagaki and his followers.

A third party was the Constitutional Imperialists. It was made up of the conservatives and, while in favor of a constitution, was opposed to any action that would weaken the power of the emperor. It favored a restricted electorate, an absolute imperial veto over all legislation, and a (bicam-:eal) two-house legislature as opposed to the more democratic one-chamber plan. It was, however, in favor of an independent judiciary, of keeping military and naval officers out of politics, and of a rather wide freedom of speech and assembly. The party itself was not permanent. Its numbers were small, but men in the government and their supporters held similar opinions, and the principles it advocated proved more influential than did those of its opponents. Many of the ideas championed by it were to be found in the finished constitution.

Following the formation of these parties there came some months of popular agitation. Each went to the nation with its views. Public mass meetings were held, and many of the radical newspapers became violent in advocating their pet theories. So disturbing were the discussions that the government felt called upon to adopt repressive measures, and by muzzling the press and public meetings it produced for a time a semblance of calm. The Japanese were as yet too unaccustomed to the institutions of the West to exercise the self-restraint in public speech that is necessary to a well-conducted popular government. They were still unprepared for the party system involved in such a constitution as that of England.

CHANGES PREPARATORY TO THE CONSTITUTION

Ito returned from his tour of the West in 1883 and almost at once changes were begun preparatory to the reorganization of the government involved in the adoption of a constitution. Of all the forms of limited monarchies he had seen, Ito was most impressed with that of Germany. He had been greatly influenced by Bismarck and by the rebirth of the Fatherland that was taking place under the empire. He felt that the spirit of the German government, with its traditions of autocratic monarchy and its bureaucracy, was more nearly that of the new Japan than was that of any other important Occidental power. His modifications of Japanese institutions clearly show how deeply he had been stirred by these convictions. He began (1884) by restoring the nobility. That of past ages had officially disappeared with the Restoration. It now seemed to Ito wise to create a new one as the preliminary to an upper house of a national legislature, and as a means of strengthening the government with the support of the more powerful, conservative classes. The orders of the new nobility, five in number, were modeled on those of Europe and were conferred on former court nobles and feudal lords of the old régime, and upon those who had been prominent in the restoration movement.

The next step was the remodeling of the cabinet to a form corresponding somewhat to that of Germany. The prime minister, like the German chancellor, was now to have the guidance of all the other ministers, and was to be responsible for the entire conduct of the administration. The bureaucracy was modified by the introduction of examinations. Official appointments to the civil service were henceforth to be made on the basis of success in examinations which were open to all subjects of the emperor. This change was eventually to make the civil bureaucracy a truly national body and was to remove it from the monopoly of the ex-samurai.

THE FRAMING AND PROMULGATION OF THE CONSTITUTION, 1889

The framing of the constitution was meanwhile under way. That task was not intrusted to a popular representative assembly. The document was to be granted by the emperor out of his own kindness, and in constructing it the nation was to have no direct voice. The work was placed in the hands of a group of men, chief of whom was Ito, who carried it on in secret, where each step in the process would not be subject to the criticism of the press. Ample time was taken, and finally, in 1889, the completed constitution was accepted by the emperor and was officially proclaimed by him amid great pomp and ceremony.

THE TERMS OF THE CONSTITUTION

The chief provisions of the document were as follows:

First, the institution of the emperor was emphasized. He was declared to be of a line that has been "unbroken from ages eternal." He was the source of all authority and combined in himself all sovereignty. He sanctioned all laws and ordered them to be proclaimed and executed. He called together and ended the Diet and dissolved the lower house. While the Diet was not sitting, he could issue ordinances which had the force of law. He was the head of the executive branch of the government, appointed and dismissed all officers, and determined their salaries. He was supreme commander of the army and navy and declared war, made peace, and concluded treaties. He conferred titles of nobility and had the power of pardoning and of granting group pardons (amnesty). He was, in other words, virtually supreme. While all these functions were in practice exercised by his ministers, the latter were responsible to him, not to the Diet, and he might interfere at any time with their actions. Still the emperor did not openly interfere in or guide the administration as did the Kaiser in Germany. In many respects he reigned but did not rule. He never under the new régime openly exercised any direct power. His official acts of importance were as a rule taken only after consultation with his privy council or his ministers. Neither was his position exactly parallel to that of the English king, for constitutionally he could act directly if he wished, and his crown was not founded upon the will of the legislature. As in feudal days all government was through the shogun, so now it was through the cabinet and the privy council. The emperor was, however, consulted as he was not in the days of the Tokugawa, and had a much larger share in the government than then.

Many rights were conceded to the subjects of the emperor. All Japanese were to be liable for taxes and military service, but, subject to the restrictions placed by law, they had equal rights to appointment to office, they could change their homes, their houses were free from search, and they had freedom of speech, public assembly, writing, association, and religion. They could be arrested only according to law and must be tried by legally appointed judges. Their property was protected, and they had the right of petition. While the recognition of these rights marked a great advance over feudal days, it must be remembered that they were far more limited than would at first appear. The fact that most of them are "subject to the restrictions placed by law" made it possible for the government to curtail them if necessary.

The Imperial Diet consisted of two chambers, the House of Peers and the House of Representatives. The first as later modified was made up of members of the imperial family and of the two higher ranks of the nobility, of representatives elected by their peers from the three lower ranks of the nobility, of distinguished men nominated by the emperor, and of some of the highest taxpayers, elected by their fellows. It was, evidently, a conservative body, and could be counted upon to check any too liberal tendencies in the lower house. The House of Representatives was made up wholly of elected members. These represented districts which theoretically were as nearly equal in population as possible. For many years the right to vote was limited by property qualifications. The Diet was to meet yearly, and the duration of the session, although it might be altered by the emperor, was fixed at three months. Members had freedom of debate and were not subject to arrest. No law could be passed without the consent of the Diet, and it might initiate legislation. The government might also initiate legislation. No new tax could be imposed without the consent of the Diet, and the annual budget must be approved by it. The Diet did not, however, have the complete power of the purse, for certain matters, the control of salaries and the expenditures of the imperial house, were outside its jurisdiction, and if it refused to pass the budget, that of the preceding year would be kept in force as the standard. The emperor had an absolute veto over legislation. The Diet had the important privilege of interpellation, or of putting questions to the different members of the cabinet. Both houses might address the crown, and by this means might present grievances and virtually impeach a minister. The Diet did not have the power that is wielded by the English Parliament. The cabinet was not responsible to it, and were it not for public opinion a stubborn emperor could almost dispense with it. Moreover, the upper house had in many matters an effective check over the lower one, and, since the former was conservative, it could prevent any radical measures from being enacted by the latter.

A Privy Council was provided for, which was a distinct body appointed by the emperor, and existed for purposes of personal consultation with him. It was made up of the distinguished statesmen of the land. Cabinet ministers were members ex-officio.

There was an institution, the Elder Statesmen, which was not provided for by the written constitution, but which was so prominent a feature of the unwritten constitution that it must be spoken of in connection with the former. The Elder Statesmen, or *Genro*, were an unofficial body made up of members of the group of *samurai* who led in the reorganization of the government. They had the ear of the emperor and by virtue of that and of their achievements occupied a commanding position in the nation. Their function was purely advisory, but in times of great national crisis they often had more weight than privy council, cabinet, or Diet. Very influential during the nineties and the first years of the twentieth century, the Elder Statesmen as an institution became extinct through the death of its members.

The cabinet had charge of the executive side of the government and was responsible to the emperor, not to the Diet. At its head was the premier, who, like his German prototype, as has been said, was its dominant figure.

A judiciary was provided for, to be filled by appointment, and to hold office during good behavior. As in some European countries, however, a separate set of courts existed for administrative cases, or those involving government officers, and over these the ordinary courts were not given jurisdiction.

The constitution was the first to be granted by a monarch of East Asia. With all its conservatism it marked the entrance of the liberal democratic theories of the West into the autocratic Far East. Then, too, although conservative, it was elastic. It was a far cry from the feudalism of 1860 to the constitutional monarchy of 1890.

The constitution so adopted had now to be put into force. It worked well. Its chief weakness, and a very real one, was the conflicts that it rendered almost inevitable between the two houses of the Diet, and especially between the lower house and the executive. With the exception of war times, when party differences were set aside in the interest of national unity, few years after 1890 passed without a struggle between the political parties and the cabinet. The former were striving to make the latter responsible to the lower house, as in England. At times they seemed to gain a measure of success, but more frequently they failed. Too often the government obtained peace and support by questionable concessions to individual members of the house.

STRUGGLE BETWEEN THE PARTIES AND THE MINISTRY

The struggle began with the preliminaries to the first Diet. The parties of the early eighties had for a time been in the background, but with the adoption of the constitution at least two were revived, the Liberals (Jiyuto) under the leadership of Itagaki, and the Liberal Conservatives (Kaishinto) directed by Okuma. Both Liberals and Liberal Conservatives demanded that the ministry be made responsible to the lower house, and formed a temporary union as an opposition party. The elections went off quietly. There was a general interest in them; in most districts three or four candidates appeared for each seat and the large majority of the half million or so to which the franchise was confined appeared at the polls. The opposition parties won a decided majority of the seats of the lower house. This, by the way, was quite representative of the various groups of the nation; the ex-samurai, while numerous, were in the minority; the leading occupations of the country were represented in about their just proportion: the lower house was not, as is the American congress, largely a body of lawyers. The upper house was, as might be expected, a conservative body.

The Diet had no sooner met than the opposition began to make trouble for the government. The budget, which by the constitution must be presented to the Diet, seemed the most promising point of attack, and on it the struggle raged furiously. Both Liberals and Liberal Conservatives saw in the partial control of the Diet over the purse their opportunity to force the ministry to its knees. The government was compelled to compromise, and granted two-thirds of the demands of the opposition. The ministry, however, while compelled to recognize the power of the parties, did not concede the main point at issue, that of responsibility to the lower house. The struggle between the legislature and the cabinet therefore did not stop, and finally in disgust the government exercised its constitutional right and in the name of the emperor dissolved the Diet.

In the elections to the second Diet the government made a determined effort to obtain control of the lower house, an act that in itself was a partial concession to the contention of the party politicians. It used every possible legal and some illegal means to insure the return of a majority of its candidates. Bribery, intimidation, and repressive laws were all employed, and the contest was marked by scenes of violence. In spite of these drastic measures, when the Diet assembled the ministry found its supporters in the House of Representatives still in the minority. In addition the government had seriously damaged its prestige by its election methods. The struggle between legislature and executive was again renewed, the chief points of attack still being financial. Upper and lower houses differed, for the upper house rather consistently sided with the government. So difficult did the ministry find its task that its reorganization became necessary, and Ito, the framer of the constitution, felt called upon to accept the premiership. This cabinet change, while caused by party opposition, was by no means made in consultation with the politicians of the lower house, and they were no more disposed to be friendly toward the new cabinet than they had been toward the old. Ito had finally to meet their demands for a curtailment of expenditures by resorting to a direct message from the emperor which announced a voluntary contribution of a tenth of the expenses of the imperial household to the defense fund of the nation, called upon all officials to make a similar sacrifice, and asked that the Diet coöperate by striving for harmony with the government. Ito further instituted extensive reductions in government expenses, and even made arrangements with Itagaki and the Liberals to obtain their support in the lower house. The result of these strenuous efforts was simply to shift the attack of the opposition groups from the budget, from which respect for the sovereign's expressed wish restrained them, to other points in the policy of the government. They were bent on hindering and irritating the government in every possible way until the principles for which they stood should be granted. Again the government was forced to confess failure, and the second Diet, like the first, was dissolved.

The third House of Representatives, elected in 1894, was, like its predecessors, in the control of the enemies of the government. Ito's agreement with the Liberals won their support, but his former followers were angered by his apparent concession to the principle of party government and went over to the opposition. Ito found that he had simply exchanged the aid of one group for that of another. The third House of Representatives, then, like its predecessors, had a nearly continuous record of disagreement with the ministry. After a bitter attack on the foreign policy of the government, and a decision to present in an address to the emperor its lack of confidence in the cabinet, the lower house, and with it the Diet, were again dissolved.

TEMPORARY PARTY TRUCE DURING THE WAR WITH CHINA

Before the new elections war had broken out with China and in that spirit of patriotism which in Japan seems always stronger than factional interests, the Diet united solidly in a cordial support of the government. Partisanship was abandoned in the enthusiasm of the war, and was not again to be displayed until after peace had been declared. The first period of struggle for a responsible ministry had come to an end. It was evident, however, that the strife would be resumed when the war was over. The only hope of lasting peace between these factions under the existing constitution was the unconditional surrender either of the liberals or of the executive. The ministry must not be thought to have been moved entirely or even primarily by selfish motives. Its leaders seem sincerely to have believed, and probably with justice, that the nation was not yet ready for a government by a cabinet responsible to a representative parliament. The further history of the struggle must, however, be deferred to a subsequent chapter.

CHAPTER IX

3. FOREIGN AFFAIRS, ECONOMIC, EDUCATIONAL, AND RE-
LIGIOUS CHANGES FROM THE RESTORATION TO THE WAR
WITH CHINA (1868–1894)

THE ESTABLISHMENT OF DIPLOMATIC RELATIONS WITH THE WEST

For the past several pages we have been discussing the change in the spirit and structure of the Japanese government made by the coming of the Westerner. This was perhaps the main feature of the years between 1853 and 1894. Of almost equal interest, however, was the development of the foreign policy of the nation. Through all but their earliest years the policy of the Tokugawa toward other countries can be summed up in one word, isolation. The coming of Perry brought this hermit existence finally to an end. It took some years to impress upon all the nation a recognition of that fact, but when once it was accepted, the necessary readjustments to the demands of the new age were made. The establishment of the diplomatic legations of Western powers in Tokyo was allowed and the young emperor on the advice of his ministers received the foreign diplomats in person and tried to maintain friendly relations between them and his administration. Japanese legations were established in the capitals of the various treaty powers, and Japan sought to conform itself to the international ways of the West.

THE GROWING SPIRIT OF NATIONALISM AND IMPERIALISM

The spirit of nationalism and patriotism which had been growing under the Tokugawa régime, and which had been roused into sudden, vigorous life by contact with the nations of the West, had expressed itself inwardly in a centralization and complete reorganization of the state. In foreign relations it showed itself in the main in three ways. The first, a passing phase, was the attempt of the conservatives to rid the nation of the foreign barbarians and to renew the policy of exclusion. This phase had practically disappeared before the seventies. The second was the rise of a spirit of imperialism, a desire to expand, which grew rapidly, and which was to have a large share in the wars and diplomacy of the eighteen nineties and the twentieth century. The third was a demand for equality with Western powers, arising from a spirit of national pride which could not stand for discrimination by any people. It showed itself principally in a demand for restored tariff and judicial power through the revision of the treaties and the abolition of extraterritoriality, and was in the twentieth century to lead to bitter resentment of the treatment of Japanese on the Pacific coast of the United States.

The spirit of imperialism first showed itself after the Meiji Restoration in a demand that all territories inhabited by Japanese, or belonging naturally to the group of Japanese islands, be occupied by the emperor's government. The belief was expressed that the Ryukyu Islands, the Bonin Islands, the Kuriles (Chishima), Karafuto (Sakhalin), and Hokkaido (Yezo), were all rightfully Japanese, and even that Korea (Chosen) should be dealt with as a subject state. Hokkaido was indisputably Japanese, and under the Tokugawa it had been held by one of the northern daimyo and the shogun. Its population was made up largely of Ainu, however, and only a few Japanese were to be found there. A special bureau was now organized by the imperial government to oversee it, and a vigorous policy of colonization and development was adopted. So successfully was the work carried on that the island speedily became a convenient outlet for the surplus population of the empire, a kind of frontier province. With Karafuto and the Kuriles the imperialistic policy was not so successful. Russia also laid claim to these territories and the controversy was settled in 1875 by an agreement whereby Japan's sovereignty over the Kuriles was to be acknowledged in return for the renunciation of all her claims to Karafuto. Karafuto, it may be added, was of strategic importance to Russia, for it commanded not only much of the shore of Eastern Siberia, but the mouth of the Amur River, the main artery of that region. The Bonin Islands were occupied without opposition in 1878.

The Ryukyu Islands presented a somewhat more difficult situation. By blood and language their inhabitants were related to the Japanese. They had been subdued by Satsuma during feudal times and for two centuries or so had been considered part of its domains. They had sent tribute embassies to China and yet as an independent state had made treaties with several Western powers. In 1868 Japan definitely claimed the islands as her own, and when in 1871 certain of their inhabitants were killed by the savages of Formosa she undertook to avenge them. Now, Formosa was a dependency of China, and Tokyo demanded redress at Peking on the ground that the men of Ryukyu were Japanese subjects. Peking both denied Japan's authority and disowned jurisdiction over the savages of Formosa. Japan replied (1874) by sending an expedition that seized and occupied southern Formosa. When China protested, Japan demanded an indemnity for her trouble. The two nations nearly came to blows, but Peking finally yielded, paid an indemnity, and the Japanese withdrew. In the meantime Japan had persuaded the king of the Ryukyu Islands to surrender his treaties with Western nations and accept her rule. She extended her provincial administration over the islands in 1879, thus making them a part of her empire. China still protested and declined to agree to a proposed division of the islands between herself and Japan, but the latter quietly persisted and succeeded in retaining possession of the entire group.

RELATIONS WITH KOREA (CHOSEN)

In Korea the situation was still more difficult. Like the Ryukyu Islands, Korea had in years past recognized the simultaneous authority of both Japan and China but was much more closely tied to China than Japan. China was nearer and more powerful, and the historic source of culture, so Korea had more respect for her. Nor had Korea for-gotten the resentment roused by the cruelties of Hideyoshi's invasion. Korea in 1868 and 1869 had refused to receive en-voys from her island neighbor. Such an attitude helped to arouse anew the Japanese desire to exert an influence in the peninsula. Moreover, some of Japan's statesmen began to fear Russian aggression, for that power had recently (1868) acquired the territory east of the Ussuri River and had estab-lished a port, Vladivostok, almost on the northern boundary of Korea. The Russians would evidently not be content to rest there in a harbor closed by ice during the winter months. Japan controlled what were virtually the only two exits from Vladivostok to the Pacific. The one, the narrow Tsugaru Strait between Hokkaido and the Main Island, was evidently Japanese. The other, the broad straits between Korea and Kyushu, had planted in their midst the two Japanese-owned islands of Tsushima and Iki. Russia once in the eighteen eighties tried to seize Tsushima but was stopped by Great

Britain. She would evidently be glad to get possession of Korea. But Korea was weak, and moreover, the country was ruled by a corrupt and inefficient government and could not, unless aided from without, hope to offer successful opposition to the great European power. The Russian might prove an

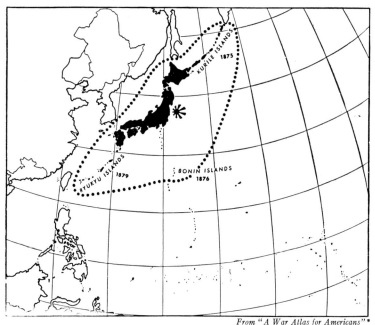

*From "A War Atlas for Americans"**

The beginning of Japanese imperialism, 1875

unpleasantly aggressive neighbor to Japan were he established on the peninsula.

One group among the Japanese leaders demanded an aggressive assertion of the interests of their country in Korea. The majority of the statesmen were unwilling, however, to commit the nation to a vigorous continental program until the work of internal reorganization should be more nearly complete. The government did not forget Korea, however.

* Prepared with the assistance of the Office of War Information. Published by Simon and Schuster.

When in 1875 a Japanese gunboat was fired on by a Korean fort the emperor's advisers decided that vigorous action was necessary. An armed expedition was sent the following year. It adopted the plan used by Perry with the shogun's officials and by tactful intimidation obtained a treaty. China, it may be added, offered no opposition when Korea negotiated the treaty as an independent power. Japan thus took the lead in opening Korea to the outside world and in its reorganization along Western lines. Treaties with Western powers followed, commerce sprang up, and a reform party came into existence.

China looked with no friendly eye upon the activity of the "island dwarfs," as she chose to call the Japanese. She was still the bulwark of Far Eastern conservatism, and naturally championed the cause of the reactionary party at Seoul, the capital of Korea. She maintained a "resident" there who, as the representative of her authority, had great influence. Japan naturally championed the reform party. Conflicts arose between the factions, and in 1882 the conservatives attacked and burned the Japanese legation and forced its inmates to flee for their lives. In return the Japanese demanded and received an indemnity and the privilege of guarding their legation with their own troops. In 1884 occurred another collision between Korean conservatives and radicals. The one called on China for assistance, the other on Japan. Both powers responded and in 1885 they agreed to withdraw their troops on the mutual written understanding that: "In case of any disturbance of grave nature occurring in Korea which might necessitate the respective countries or either sending troops, it is hereby understood that each shall give to the other previous notice in writing of its intention to do so and that after the matter is settled they shall withdraw their troops." Affairs in the peninsula temporarily quieted down, but the friction between reformers and reactionaries continued and was to lead in 1894 to war between Japan and China.

TARIFF AND LEGAL READJUSTMENTS

The agitation for the revision of the foreign treaties grew out of Japan's loss of the judicial and financial power embodied in them. When the treaties were negotiated the Japanese laws were still what they had been in feudal days, and the powers did not think it just to subject their citizens to them or to the local courts. Each Western nation stipulated that all cases in which its subjects or citizens were defendants should be tried by its consuls and under its own laws. The residence of foreigners was restricted to certain specified "treaty ports." This "extraterritoriality" was in force in China and Turkey and wherever Western nations were in treaty relations with a non-Christian state. Tariff duties, as in China, were also made a matter of formal agreement: otherwise they might be subject to frequent modifications. The Japanese felt that extraterritoriality and the sacrifice of tariff control were a mark of inferiority. This the patriotic spirit of the nation could not willingly tolerate. Moreover, under extraterritoriality wrongs committed by foreigners to Japanese frequently went unpunished, and too many consular courts, especially of the smaller nations, were poorly administered. Japan was in great need of revenue, and felt keenly the curtailment of her rights to raise it from tariffs, another reason for treaty revision.

One of the first acts of the government of the Restoration was to plan for the removal of these restrictions, and in 1871 an embassy was sent to Europe and America to ask for it. Such a concession had never been granted by Christian nations to a non-Christian power and since Japanese laws and law courts were yet to be reorganized, the failure of the mission was certain before it started. The agitation, however, had only begun. In 1878 the United States agreed to a treaty on the terms desired by Tokyo, but the document was not to go into force unless the other powers made similar concessions. This Europe was unwilling to do. Then the Japanese foreign office tried conferences with the Tokyo representatives of the powers. Two of these gatherings were held, one in 1882 and another in 1886, but both failed. Japan seemed to Westerners still unprepared to be trusted with full control over the lives and property of strangers. In the meantime the Japanese thinking public had taken up the agitation, and from the early eighties tariff control and the abolition of extraterritoriality were vigorously demanded both from the press and the public platform. Halfway measures were denounced. A compromise agreed to by the 1886 conference of the representatives of the powers and favored by the government would have extended the jurisdiction of Japanese courts to foreigners, provided that all cases in which Westerners were involved should be submitted to courts to which foreign judges had been appointed. This concession the Japanese public would not tolerate.

Hand in hand with the demand for treaty revision went an earnest attempt so to conform national institutions to Western standards that all reasons for discrimination would cease to exist. European customs and dress were copied. The new education was promoted. The formation of laws on Western models was pushed. A new civil code was compiled on the general lines in use in the West. A code of commercial law was drawn up resembling closely that of Germany, and French models were followed in framing the criminal law. Judges, appointed from those specially trained for the profession, were to serve during life or good behavior. In 1890 the codes were finally approved by the emperor.

The reasons for extraterritoriality were fast ceasing to exist and the powers could evidently not long, with any show of justice, continue to maintain it. In 1888, Mexico signed a treaty granting to Japan judicial control, and the United States had long been known to be willing to take a similar step as soon as the leading European powers would agree to do so. The lower house of the Diet kept urging the ministry to push the negotiations, and the government took the question directly to the European capitals. Finally in 1894, Great Britain, whose trade was larger and whose subjects resident in Japan were more numerous and more opposed to a change than those of any other Western power, signed a treaty drawn in the revised form desired by Japan, and the United States followed. The other powers conformed in the course of the next three years. Japan had so effectively demonstrated her complete reorganization that further delay would have been unjust. In 1899, extraterritoriality in Japan came to an end, consular courts and foreign "settlements" were abolished, and Westerners became subject to Japanese courts and laws. Tariff autonomy or self-control was partly restored in 1899, although it did not completely go into effect until more than a decade later (1911). For the first time in history an Asiatic country was admitted to the circle of Western powers on the basis of full equality. The concession was a notable achievement for Japanese patriotism and ability.

The political reorganization and the assumption of a new international status were the most prominent features of the years between the coming of Perry and 1894. The changes in the structure, policies, and position of the state, were, however, only part of the transformations in progress in all phases of the nation's life. Impact with the West was producing a revolution in commerce, finance, transportation, industry, dress, thought, education, and religion, in some of its phases more complete than that made by the coming of Buddhism and Chinese culture over a thousand years before.

As in that earlier transition period, the government led, but also as then, the people followed, in time with enthusiasm.

ECONOMIC REORGANIZATION

Commerce, naturally, sprang up almost as soon as the Perry treaty had been signed. Naturally, too, it was many years before it attained large proportions. The nation had so long been closed to the outer world that it took time to develop a demand for foreign goods and the ability to pay for those purchased. Until at least 1881, the balance of trade was against Japan, and she was drained of her currency. After 1887 commerce grew more rapidly, thanks partly to a more active supervision by the government and partly to the internal reorganization of the industry of the country. Its period of greatest increase was to be after the war with China. During its earlier years this revived commerce was largely under the control of the foreign middleman. It was he who came to Japan, purchased goods from the local merchants, and exported these products to other lands. In many instances the middleman was not an ideal representative of the West. Adventurers who had followed the flags of foreign powers tried to exploit the new Japan to their own advantage. The Japanese had been unaccustomed to foreign commerce and time was required to produce an adequate machinery to handle it. The government tried to help, but in the early days many of the Japanese merchants who dealt with the foreigner followed his business methods, and a report of Japanese commercial dishonesty became current. While conditions later improved, the story still spread, for there was some basis for it. It lost nothing in the telling and gave the average Westerner an impression that Japanese business men were unreliable.

With the growth of commerce, banks naturally sprang up. At first the government experimented with various devices, and in 1873 established a national banking system patterned largely after that in use in the United States. The country was being drained of its metal currency, however, and the banks and the national treasury were in a precarious state. In 1881 the government was led to organize a great central institution, later the Bank of Japan, and, to assist in trade and foreign exchange, a secondary institution, later the Yokohama Specie Bank. Through the latter it took over for a time the foreign commerce of the country and by an ingenious device built up a metal reserve and made possible the resumption of specie payments. Postal savings banks were introduced. Before 1900 the system finally took the form whose main features it long continued to preserve, a national Bank of Japan which alone issued notes, and centering in it a system of private, joint-stock concerns. There were to be added in the years after 1894 agricultural and industrial banks for the aid of farmers and manufacturers. As in most branches of the nation's life, laws and state supervision carefully regulated all private financial institutions.

With the growth of commerce came, too, an improvement in means of transportation. Steamships plied the coastal waters of the islands. At first most of them were built abroad and were the property of foreigners, but before long they began to be constructed and owned at home. Here again the government gave its encouragement, and heavily subsidized companies laid the basis for the tremendous growth of the twentieth century in domestic and foreign shipping. The state was a pioneer in railway building. In spite of earnest opposition by the conservatives a line was begun between Tokyo and its port, Yokohama, and was officially opened by the emperor in 1872. The state continued to promote railways and most of the earlier ones were constructed either by it or by government-aided companies. Later the privately owned lines predominated, but, as we shall see, they were nationalized during more recent years. Telegraph lines were built by the state and in 1886 were united with the postal service under a joint bureau. The telephone was introduced in 1877.

In industry the state again had a prominent part, and owned directly many different plants. By 1890 there were over two hundred steam factories in the country and the ancient handicrafts were beginning to be supplanted by the methods of the industrial revolution. The great industrial development of the nation, however, was not to take place until after the war with China.

The government led, too, in bettering agriculture. After the Meiji Restoration the peasant was made the owner of the soil that he had cultivated for the feudal lords under the old régime, and payment of taxes in money was substituted for forced labor and for payment in the products of the soil. Western agricultural experts were brought in to suggest improvements in the time-honored methods of the farmer, and new breeds of cattle and horses were introduced.

In the reorganization of banking, commerce, transportation, industry, and agriculture, then, the state, directed by the reformers, had a major part. For this there were two reasons. First, the state was the only institution which had the organization, the capital, and the credit to undertake operations on the large scale necessary for successful competition with the industrialized West. At the coming of Perry there were few if any large commercial fortunes in the country, capital was in land, and industry and trade were crude and without an organization fitted to cope with that of the West. In the second place, an emphasis upon the state had been encouraged by the Tokugawa shoguns, for they sought to exercise a supervision over all the life of the nation. It was but natural that the ministers of the Restoration should follow the precedent of past ages.

EDUCATIONAL AND RELIGIOUS TRANSFORMATION

The government led the way in remaking the educational system of the land. Before the downfall of the shogunate, Japanese students had begun to find their way to the West, partly on their own initiative, and partly with the help of the state. With the Meiji Restoration scores of students went to Europe and America to drink of the new learning at its sources. They returned bursting with ideas and became ardent supporters and leaders of the reform movement. The embassy that in 1871 went abroad to ask for a revision of the treaties came back with the determination to start a modern school system, and in 1872 a law was passed which was the basis of universal compulsory primary education. A complete program of public instruction was gradually carried out, beginning with the elementary school and leading through the "middle" and "high" schools, to the national universities. Enthusiastic private effort supplemented that of the state, and Christian missionary institutions added their contribution. Foreign teachers were engaged, among them some who later not only interpreted the West to Japan, but Japan to the West. Translations of Western books were made.

Japan had been opened by America and many of her youth were there in school. England was the great commercial power of the Far East. It was but natural then, that English should be studied extensively and should be the language through which the Japanese chose to acquire Western learning. Fresh combinations of the convenient Chinese characters were formed to express the new ideas that were constantly pouring in. Newspapers sprang into existence, some of them encouraged by the state, but many of them edited by men who had been too recently introduced to Western thought and institutions to have their radicalism balanced with the sound judgment born of experience. So numerous and influential did such papers become that by the eighties the government found it necessary to curb them with press laws. A simpler form of literary style appeared and a beginning was made toward conforming the language of the printed page more nearly to the Japanese everyday speech. Education and the new ideas were being brought to the man on the street.

Even in religion changes were being made. By their experiences of the sixteenth and seventeenth centuries the Japanese had been taught to view Christianity with mingled fear, contempt, and hate. The rigid prohibitions against it remained on the public edict-boards until 1873 and complete religious toleration was not granted until after the introduction of the constitution. Under the shelter of the treaty ports, however, missionary activity was begun by foreign representatives of Protestant, Russian, and Roman Catholic communions, and the foundations of the church were laid anew. A number of notably able men were among the missionary pioneers, and had a share in remolding not only the religious thought but other phases of national life. In the eighties, when all things foreign shared in the popularity that attended the national enthusiasm for transformation, the Christian church grew rapidly. The centuries of prejudice could not be entirely forgotten, however. A reaction took place during the nineties and Christianity for a while gained ground but slowly.

CHARACTERISTICS OF THE TRANSITION PERIOD

To the traveler or foreign resident in Japan the years of marked transition were at times amusing, at times bewildering, and always interesting. With the great alterations in political institutions, in commerce, transportation, industry, education, thought, and religion, there were other changes, some of them much more superficial, but all of them significant. A mixture of costumes was to be found, often ludicrous. To Japanese houses were added foreign rooms fitted out with European furniture. Business blocks and public buildings were erected either in an avowedly foreign architectural style, or in a curious mixture that was neither Occidental nor Oriental and that tried to be both. The nation was attempting to find itself, to adjust itself to the new world.

By 1894 the crisis of the transition period had passed. The government had been completely reorganized and a constitution had been given several years of trial. An army and navy had been built up after approved Western models. A modern school system was in successful operation. Tariff and judicial autonomy were on the point of being granted. Industry and commerce were giving promise of vigorous life. The reorganization was not complete and its fruits were only beginning to be seen, but in the main the shock caused by internal adaptation to the modern world was over. From 1894 on, the reorganized Japan was to expand and take her place as an increasingly important member in the family of nations.

CHAPTER X

1894 TO 1937: JAPAN TAKES HER PLACE AMONG THE
POWERS OF THE WORLD

I. THE WAR WITH CHINA, THE BOXER UPRISING, AND THE
WAR WITH RUSSIA (1894–1905)

JAPAN'S INTEREST IN FOREIGN AFFAIRS AFTER 1894

By 1894, as we have seen, the work of the internal reorganization of Japan had been brought to a point where it
no longer needed the entire attention of the nation, and
where it was not only safe but necessary to take a more
active part in international affairs. The new Japan entered
into a period of expansion in population, industry, and commerce. This expansion, together with her intense patriotism
and the existing conditions in the Orient, was certain to
bring on serious clashes with other countries. The first
trouble was in Korea, and out of it was to come a long train
of events which has been momentous for the entire world.

That there should be friction in Korea seemed inevitable.
Here, it will be recalled, China and Japan had temporarily
adjusted their differences by the agreement of 1885, but
both had continued their plots. In the background was
Russia which, as Japan's statesmen well knew, was more to
be feared than China. Unless heroic measures were taken,
the feeble and reactionary Korea would fall an easy prey to
the Russians. If Korea became Russian, Japan believed
that she would have a relentlessly aggressive power at her
very doors, that her commerce with the neighboring conti-

nent would be cut off by unfavorable restrictions, and that a possible outlet of her growing population would be threatened. We have already seen that Czarist Russia desired a foothold in southern Korea to make sure of a safe passage from Vladivostok to the open Pacific. She would undoubtedly welcome the acquisition of ice-free ports in Korea or North China as outlets to Siberian railways and trade routes, and as open doors to the commercial and naval control of the Far East. She was already plotting in Korea and was so strong in Peking that she might succeed in using China as a cat's-paw. Japan, as yet not certain of herself, feared the Russian menace, and sought to strengthen the hands of the reform party in Korea in its attempts to reorganize the inefficient and corrupt government and make it capable of holding its own against foreign aggressors.

WAR WITH CHINA OVER KOREA, 1894–1895

Between the reactionaries, supported by China, and the reformers, encouraged by Japan, there were frequent clashes, and the Korean government became, if possible, more hopelessly useless than ever. The agreement of 1885 could not be a permanent settlement of the difficulty, for the joint interests it recognized could only lead to further friction. China treated Korea as a tributary, scorning the Japanese contention that she was independent. Friction increased, and finally, when a rebellion broke out, China sent troops to suppress it and announced her action to Japan. She did not strictly obey the letter of the convention of 1885, for the notice was sent after and not before the troops were dispatched. When the Chinese action became known, Japan promptly prepared to send a force to Korea and notified China to that effect. Although the rebellion that had been the occasion for sending the troops quickly died down, Japan and China both kept their forces in Korea. Japan proposed that China unite with her in permanently reorganizing the peninsula's government and in putting down disorder. China declined, refusing to admit that Korea was independent, and claimed the right to fix limits both to the number of Japanese troops that could be sent, and to their use. China evidently suspected the Japanese of a desire to control the peninsula and intended to assert unmistakably her own exclusive authority over the land.

Japan was at that time in the midst of a bitter struggle between the lower house of the Diet and the ministry, and China evidently thought her too torn by internal quarrels to be ready for war. She had, moreover, a profound contempt for these "island dwarfs" who had once copied her civilization and had now partly abandoned it for that of the West. China began sending more troops to Korea, although she had been warned by Tokyo that such action would mean war. While one group of reënforcements was on its way, an armed clash occurred with the naval forces of the Japanese. War followed (July, 1894).

To China's surprise the Japanese ceased their internal dissensions, and suddenly became solidly united. They enthusiastically supported the emperor's forces. The ministry was possibly not at all unwilling to turn the current of popular thought from the struggle for a responsible cabinet to imperialism. Indeed, some have claimed to see in the war a clever ruse of the government to withdraw the attention of the nation from the constitutional struggle by a policy of foreign expansion.

The Chinese were beaten on land and sea. Their navy, made up of modern ships, was decisively defeated and its remnants were sunk or captured. Port Arthur and Talien, naval stations on the Liaotung Peninsula, and commanding South Manchuria, were captured. Both places had been fortified under the direction of European engineers, and

Port Arthur, with its splendid natural harbor, was considered especially strong. Mukden, the capital of Manchuria, was threatened; Wei-hai-wei, the great harbor-fortress of Shantung, was taken. Japan thus dominated the naval approaches to North China and Peking. A successful expedition was sent to Formosa and the neighboring Pescadores Islands. China was compelled to sue for peace. By the treaty (of Shimonoseki, April, 1895) that ended the war, the complete independence of Korea was formally acknowledged (by China only); the Liaotung Peninsula in Southern Manchuria was ceded to Japan; Formosa and the Pescadores were given her; a large indemnity (about $150,000,000) was to be paid her; and China agreed to open up the Yangtze River and certain additional treaty ports to the trade of the world. The dwarf had worsted the giant, and had demonstrated that it was a factor to be reckoned with in the Far East.

Europe had watched the war with interest and surprise, and some of the powers viewed the outcome with alarm. Russia saw her plans for southern expansion blocked and her influence in North China threatened. The German emperor saw in Japan's victory the beginning of the military rebirth of Eastern Asia and feared that a yellow wave of conquest would eventually shake to its foundations European world-supremacy. Even before the treaty of peace had been negotiated it seems that Russia had given assurance to China that Japan would not be allowed to retain the Liaotung Peninsula. As might have been expected, soon after the treaty was signed, Russia, seconded by her ally, France, lodged protests in Tokyo. These were courteous, but firm, for they said that the terms of the treaty threatened the peace of the Far East. At the same time Germany presented a note with a similar purport, but curt and offensive in its language and in the method chosen for transmission. The only course open to Japan was compliance. She had no ally and could not hope to resist successfully the armed forces of the three powers. With as good face as was possible under the circumstances she "accepted the advice," and gave back to China the Liaotung Peninsula in return for an additional indemnity.

The Japanese public was bitterly disappointed with the outcome of the war. To many the original treaty had seemed too mild. Then came the return of the Liaotung Peninsula, a blow to the national pride as severe as it was unexpected. A conflict between Japan and Russia became almost inevitable. The ministry at once began a policy of naval and military expansion. Taxes were increased and sums far larger than the indemnity received from China were spent in preparation for the coming struggle. Japan's leaders saw that if she was to win from European powers a voice in Far Eastern affairs, she must have an effective armament.

With the growth of the army and navy, the position of the Satsuma and Choshu groups was strengthened. The ex-samurai of these former fiefs of the South had succeeded in controlling the fighting arms of the nation, and now with the great program of preparedness, exerted a much stronger influence than formerly over all the policies of the government. They stood, very naturally, for territorial expansion and for a vigorous policy on the continent. They had much opposition, as we shall see a little later, but the force of events aided them in committing Japan to a policy of imperialism.

The war with China impressed on the world the importance and the thoroughness of the transformation that had been wrought in Japan in the preceding forty years. The Japanese had demonstrated their ability to use the weapons and organization of the West.

Japan was not, however, to attain easily recognition of her claim to a voice in the affairs of China, to a predominant interest in Korea, and to an open door into Manchuria. As a reward for her interference in 1895, Russia was given by China the privilege of building the trans-Siberian railway that was to bind together her Siberian and European possessions, directly across Northern Manchuria to Vladivostok. This would, of course, give the Czar a decided hold on Northern Manchuria, which was admittedly Chinese territory. Russia guaranteed a loan raised in Paris by China to pay off the indemnity due Japan, an act which might be the precedent for a financial protectorate over China and which at least seemed to impose a debt of gratitude to Russia. Russian plots continued in Korea and served greatly to embarrass the Japanese. The latter, in fact, played directly into the hands of Russia by a bungling management of their interests in Korea. The Japanese agent was implicated in an attack on the royal palace that resulted in the murder of Korea's queen and the king's escape to the Russian legation, where he lived for two years. Many Japanese merchants and settlers in the peninsula needlessly antagonized the Koreans by an overbearing attitude, dishonest business dealings, and even violence. Japan had good reason to fear that the agents of Russia would obtain more than a passing hold on Korea, and from that vantage point embarrass Japan's commerce with the continent and threaten her coasts.

Then in 1897 began a scramble of European powers for leased territories and "spheres of influence" in China. In the last quarter of the nineteenth century Western nations were entering on a new period of colonial expansion. Africa had recently been divided, unclaimed islands of the sea were being occupied, and the territorial integrity of all weak nations was threatened. China's weakness had been made unmistakably apparent in her war with Japan, and European powers were not slow to take advantage of it. In 1897,

Germany took advantage of the murder of some of her subjects — missionaries — by a Chinese mob, and demanded a ninety-nine year lease on the strategic harbor of Kiaochow in the province of Shantung, where the outrage had taken place. Here she began building a model city, Tsingtao, and

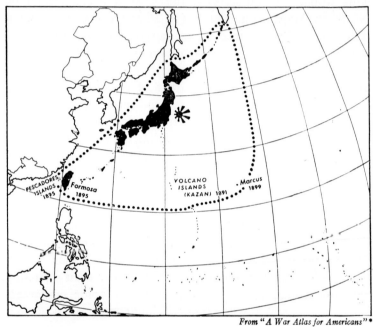

From "*A War Atlas for Americans*" *

Japanese Expansion, including China-Japanese War, 1894–95.

connected it with the interior by railway lines for which she had been granted concessions. She was given the privilege, too, of working the valuable coal mines of the province.

A little later Russia, as compensation, demanded and obtained a lease on Port Arthur and Dairen on that Liaotung Peninsula of which she had deprived Japan scarcely three years before. She connected them with the Siberian railway

* Prepared with the assistance of the Office of War Information. Published by Simon and Schuster.

by a branch line. A Russo-Chinese bank was established, as a joint enterprise of the two nations, as the name indicates, but with the first-named partner predominant. Russia had thus obtained what was for most of the year an ice-free port for her Siberian railway and was in a position to dominate all Manchuria and North China. She could block Japanese commercial and industrial expansion by closing the ports of Manchuria to all non-Russian trade. And this she tried to do. Great Britain at the same time obtained a lease on Wei-hai-wei, the fortified harbor that commanded the approach to Peking from the Shantung side, and marked out for herself a "sphere of influence" in the Yangtze Valley within which she was to have the preference in commerce and in providing capital for railways, industry, and mines. France was given a lease and a sphere of influence in South China. Neither Great Britain nor France were as yet to be serious rivals of Japan, however.

JAPAN'S PART IN REPRESSING THE BOXER OUTBREAK

Following this "leasing" of her territory and the partitioning of the empire into spheres of influence there was a reform movement in China. Led by the young emperor, the progressives made a serious effort to reorganize their nation, as Japan had done, by adopting Western methods. A reaction followed which ended in the uprising of 1900, an armed attempt, led by a conservative party called the Boxers and sanctioned by the dowager empress, to rid the land of the Westerner. The foreign residents in Peking were attacked in the legation quarter and Christian missionaries and their converts were killed in exposed stations throughout North China. The powers formed an international army. Japan joined in a relief expedition that rescued foreigners in Peking, and as a result gained a voice in international councils over Chinese affairs.

EVENTS PRECEDING THE RUSSO-JAPANESE WAR

Russia had taken advantage of the Boxer disturbances to rush troops into Manchuria, to protect her citizens and her property. After the uprising was over, she still maintained her forces in that region and seemed determined on a permanent occupation. Japan protested, and the United States, newly aroused to an interest in the Far East by her entrance into the Philippines in 1898, attempted to insure in Manchuria, as elsewhere in China, the principle of territorial integrity and the "open door" policy, or equal economic and political privileges for the citizens of all nations. Russia promised to remove her troops. In reality she had no serious intention of yielding and sought an agreement with China which would have turned Manchuria into a Russian province and which failed only because of the strong protests of the United States, Great Britain, and Japan. She did, however, obtain special privileges in the region and in 1903 appointed a "viceroy" to administer her interests on the Amur and in Manchuria, treating the latter region almost as though it were already her own.

It became increasingly evident to Japan that she must fight. Russia seemingly had no intention of withdrawing from Manchuria and declined to recognize the Japanese claim to a voice in the affairs of that district. Should she stay she would probably succeed in keeping the door closed and in crippling the growth of Japanese commerce. She would certainly threaten Japanese interests in Korea. Japan sought to avoid an appeal to arms. She tried negotiations, but the Russians would not concede that she had any right to be heard in Manchurian questions, and although they acknowledged that she had special interests in Korea, they insisted on placing restrictions on her control of that kingdom. Japan would probably have welcomed an alliance with Russia had the latter been willing to make what seemed to Tokyo a fair division of influence in the Far East.

Foreseeing the approaching conflict, Japan continued to strengthen her army and navy and entered into a pact with Great Britain. This Anglo-Japanese Alliance, concluded early in 1902, was limited in its scope to China and Korea, and recognized the special interests of Great Britain in China and of Japan in China and Korea. It provided that in case either ally went to war with another power to defend these interests the other would remain neutral and would use its influence to keep other powers from attacking its ally. In case one or more additional powers were to join in the hostilities against one ally, the other agreed to come to its assistance. The two were to make war and peace together. The agreement was to be in force for five years. England was beginning to see threatened the dominant commercial position she had held in China in the earlier years of the nineteenth century and especially feared Russian aggression. She was quite willing to see Japan attack her rival. The agreement was, however, chiefly of benefit to Japan, for it gave her the prestige of alliance with the leading financial, naval, and commercial power of the world, and virtually insured the isolation of Russia in the coming struggle. Other European powers would probably not care to join the Czar at the expense of a war with England. It gave to Japan, too, the much needed support of the London bankers.

THE RUSSO-JAPANESE WAR, 1904–1905

Even with the British alliance the outcome of a war with Russia was by no means a certain victory for Japan, and the latter sought by long negotiations to avoid war. Russia persistently refused to grant Japan's demands and seemingly held her in contempt. The Japanese offered to recognize Manchuria as outside their sphere of influence providing Russia would similarly state that Korea was outside her own sphere. This Russia refused to do. Russian activities on the southern coast and northern frontiers of Korea convinced Tokyo that the imperialists in charge of the Czar's government were engaged in a deliberately aggressive policy in the peninsula itself. From Japan's standpoint the only alternative was war. Both powers had been actively preparing but Japan obtained the initial advantage by a prompt attack following the severance of diplomatic relations but without a declaration of war (February, 1904).

Hostilities continued for over a year. Russia fought under a handicap. The field of battle was thousands of miles from her European possessions, the source of most of her men and supplies and the only connecting link was a single-track railway. Her administration, particularly of her navy, was handicapped by corruption and incompetency. The Japanese were near home and were well organized and led. Their ability and efficiency were the surprise of the neutral world. The Russian armies resisted stubbornly but were steadily driven back. The Czar's fleets, which might have imperiled Japan's communication with her armies on the continent, were destroyed or penned up in Port Arthur. Port Arthur itself was captured after a desperate resistance, and a few weeks later Mukden, the capital of Manchuria, fell before the Japanese attack. The Baltic fleet, after a famous cruise around the Cape of Good Hope, was destroyed in the Straits of Tsushima between Japan and Korea in the "Battle of the Sea of Japan." The Japanese command of the eastern seas could no longer be endangered. In spite of her reverses Russia was by no means crushed: but for internal disturbances she might still have persisted and won. The war was, however,

CHAPTER XI

1894 TO 1937: JAPAN TAKES HER PLACE AMONG THE
POWERS OF THE WORLD

2. FROM THE TREATY OF PORTSMOUTH (1905) TO 1937

REORGANIZATION OF POSSESSIONS AND DEPENDENCIES

After the treaty of Portsmouth, Japanese statesmen set themselves to the task of organizing their territorial acquisitions in a way that would repay the nation for the great sacrifices entailed by the two wars. Formosa, of course, had been theirs since 1895. It had been one thing, however, to take it from China, and another to occupy it and make of it a profitable colony. Its west coast was inhabited by Chinese who resented the transfer to new masters and offered them armed resistance. When this was put down, the Japanese faced the more serious enemy of disease, for the land had been notoriously unhealthful and the Chinese population had been maintained only by continued immigration from the mainland. Japanese doctors succeeded in reducing the death rate by modern sanitation and medicine. The eastern section of the island was mountainous and was inhabited by savage tribes of head-hunters. Some of these the Japanese induced to settle down and become peaceful agriculturalists. Others were restricted to increasingly narrow localities by drastic police measures and constant vigilance. Japanese administration in its initial stages was corrupt.

For years Formosa was a drain on the imperial treasury. Eventually, as order was restored, new industries were in-

troduced and old ones improved, railways were built, administrative efficiency was increased, and the island ceased to
be a dead weight on the nation and became more nearly a
contributor to its wealth. Irrigation was encouraged and
the valuable forests were conserved and improved. The
administration encouraged the three great staple crops, tea
(in the northern part of the island), rice (in the center), and
sugar (in the south). The production of sugar was especially
aided, for practically all of Japan's supply is imported. Education was encouraged. The colonial officials made an eager
and careful study of European colonial administrations and
tried to raise the standard of living of islanders.

In 1905 Korea theoretically still had her independence.
That had been recognized by Japan on several occasions,
and it was to insure it that the war with China had been
waged. Had the Koreans been able to take steps vigorously
and promptly to reorganize the administration and to insure
the independence of the country against European and
Chinese aggression, it is quite possible that Japan would
have withdrawn its hand. Japan felt, however, that Korea
could not be trusted to manage its own affairs. There were,
it is true, a few earnest and patriotic Korean reformers who
might in time have worked out the salvation of their land;
but Japan, after her experiences of the past several decades,
was not disposed to grant them a free hand. She had not
fought two wars to maintain her interests in the neighboring peninsula, to risk them to the control of a feeble monarch, a corrupt court, and a few untried and possibly erratic
reformers. Moreover, her imperialistic ambitions had been
aroused. Almost immediately after the treaty of Portsmouth, she obtained the unwilling assent of Korea to a
treaty which turned over to her the control of the foreign
affairs of the peninsular kingdom and provided for a Japanese resident-general to supervise the administration. This

agreement partly nullified the independence that had been repeatedly recognized by Japan, and endangered the treaty rights of other powers. But Europe and America consented to the change, and Korean patriots, however bitter they might feel, could not hope to resist successfully. Ito undertook to fill the post of resident-general. He attempted still to preserve the native court and administrative machinery, and at the same time to parallel it with a system of Japanese advisers and to reform completely the finance, police, laws, administration of justice, education, sanitation, industry, and commerce of the land. The dual system of government was at best a clumsy one. Korean officialdom could not be cleared of inefficiency and corruption in a day, and coöperated sullenly or not at all. The Japanese were heartily disliked by the Koreans as a whole. The inevitable friction between the two peoples was increased by the high-handed action of many Japanese officials and immigrants, who looked upon the peninsula as conquered territory and a legitimate field for exploitation. There was in Japan, moreover, a strong party of imperialists who desired the complete annexation of the country. The form of dual government was maintained about four years, but in August, 1910, Korea formally signed a treaty that annexed her to Japan. Under the old name of Chosen, Korea was made an integral part of the empire.

The Tokyo statesmen tried to increase the wealth of the land and to insure the Japanization, if one may use that term, of the Koreans. Robbery was reduced, railway and highway construction promoted, agricultural experiment stations were multiplied, much-needed forestry programs were undertaken, and industry was encouraged. By the treaty of annexation, the retired royal house was pensioned and honored and Koreans were promised official positions if they were loyal and competent. Japan wished the Koreans to become loyal subjects of the emperor. She hoped, too, that as rapidly as possible they would become pro-Japanese. To promote this, Japanese laws and law courts were extended to the peninsula, many schools were founded, and the use of the Japanese language was encouraged.

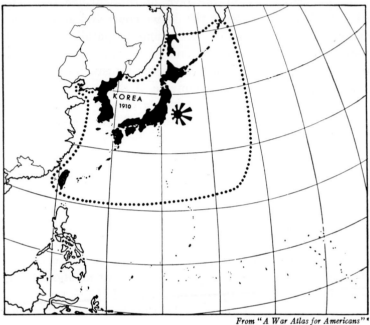

Korea's turn in 1910

The Koreans hardly faced the prospect of assimilation with complete pleasure. There were deep undercurrents of discontent. Christian missions, begun long before annexation, prospered as they had in no other Far Eastern land in the nineteenth century, and the Japanese, fearing lest revolt should cloak itself with religion and seek refuge in the church, have naturally been suspicious of the influence of the foreign pastor over his flock. At times friction occurred, notably

* Prepared with the assistance of the Office of War Information.   Published by Simon and Schuster.

over the state supervision of missionary schools, and over the trial of a number of native Christians, most of them innocent, on the charge of plotting against the government. Following World War I, in 1919, due partly to the influence of President Wilson's speeches and to the severity of the Japanese rule, there was an attempt to overthrow this authority. The disturbances were repressed with a firm hand, and then, by adopting a much more conciliatory policy, the government sought to prevent future uprisings. By such rule the mass of the Koreans have suffered from a standard of living even lower than that of the Japanese. Many thousands have sought relief by emigration to Japan proper, to Manchuria, and to Eastern Siberia.

Sakhalin, or Karafuto as it is called by the Japanese, which lies to the north of Japan's main islands, did not prove a very profitable acquisition. In the southern half, the section ceded by Russia in the treaty of Portsmouth, there are several hundred square miles of arable lands, and a few thousand Japanese came in and settled on them. The fisheries are the most important income producing feature of the island. The forests are also an important source of revenue, and there are rich veins of coal. The territory was, however, relatively undeveloped.

JAPAN'S GROWING INTEREST AND POWER IN MANCHURIA

In Manchuria Japan's position was not as strong as in Korea nor her policy as clearly indicated for her by local conditions. She had gone to war with Russia ostensibly to defend the open door and the integrity of China. By the fortunes of war, she found herself on the conclusion of peace in the possession of the very Russian holdings in South Manchuria against the use of which she had protested. Consistency and loyalty to pledges repeatedly made in treaties and conventions with various powers demanded that she respect

Chinese sovereignty and the principle of equal economic opportunity for all. Many Japanese felt, however, that the war had so altered conditions that a strict adherence to promises made earlier should not be insisted upon. The Japanese desired to use for their own advantage the territory taken at the cost of war. Moreover, the successes of the war had strengthened the imperialistic ambitions of the nation.

Manchuria was a tempting field of expansion. It bordered on Korea; it was possessed of immense resources of field, mine, and forest; it was still a frontier country; it had been an integral part of China proper for less than three centuries and only recently had the Chinese entered it in large numbers. It was now being rapidly settled by Chinese who were demonstrating by the results of their farming the immense fertility of the land. Japan's population was steadily increasing. In 1891 it had been 40,718,677, in 1899, 44,260,652, in 1903, 46,732,876 and by 1908 it was to be 49,588,804, and by 1919, 57,233,906. The arable land of the islands was not all occupied, but the limit was in sight. The pressure of population must be relieved either by emigration or by promoting industry and the exchange of its products abroad for food. In either case Manchuria appeared to the Japanese as a promising market, and its mines, forests, and fields were sources of abundant raw materials.

AMERICANS AND THE MANCHURIAN RAILWAYS

There were efforts to loosen Japan's hold on Manchuria. The ink was hardly dry on the treaty of Portsmouth before the American railway genius, Harriman, had agreed with the Tokyo authorities to buy the roads that had been taken from Russia. He planned to obtain control of the trans-Siberian road, to span the Atlantic and Pacific with steamship lines, and thus to belt the world with a transportation system controlled by himself. This arrangement, however, stood in the way of Japanese expansion, and while favored by Ito was set aside on the advice of the Japanese chief commissioner to Portsmouth. Both British and American financiers sought from China railway concessions in both the Japanese and Russian spheres of influence. Harriman negotiated for the lines in Manchuria still held by Russia. The United States through Secretary P. C. Knox proposed a plan for the neutralization of the railways of Manchuria. The powers were jointly to lend China money to purchase the existing Russian and Japanese lines and to construct such additional roads as might be needed. The administration of the roads was to be for a time in the hands of an international commission. The plan was significant, for had it been carried out, it would have meant a precedent for the substitution of a benevolent international protectorate over China for "spheres of influence," "leased territories," "special interests," and other forms under which each nation was trying to obtain for its exclusive enjoyment some part of the country. If successful, this plan would have lessened intrigues and reduced causes of friction and war. To the American proposal Japanese and Russian expansionists could hardly be expected to agree, and since they were in control at their respective capitals, alarm at the threatened action led the two countries not only to disapprove publicly of the plan, but to enter into an agreement (1910) to act jointly to conserve and coördinate their interests in Manchuria. The former enemies had been driven together by the American suggestion and their common interests.

The temptation was great to obtain special privileges for Japanese merchants as well as for Japanese railroads. The accusation was repeatedly made that by manipulation of the customs, railroad rebates, preferential rates of interest in the Manchurian branches of the Yokohama Specie Bank, and the evasion of taxes, the Japanese were obtaining favors for their own goods and merchants at the expense of those of other powers. In some instances the complaints may have been well-founded, but if there was a violation of the open door it was more by indirect than by direct methods.

JAPAN'S INTEREST IN CHINA TO 1914

Japan's interest in China was not confined to Manchuria and events were soon to take place which would give her a larger voice in the affairs of her huge neighbor. If Manchuria was a rich field for commercial, mining, and industrial exploitation, China proper was even more so. There was a huge industrious and thrifty population, potentially the greatest market in the world. There were great supplies of raw material and of coal and iron, of the last of which an industrial Japan, without much iron ore of her own, stood particularly in need. There was a natural field for commercial expansion.

By every device known to industry and commerce Japan's trade with China was encouraged. Heavily subsidized steamers plied the waters of the Yangtze and its tributaries; Japanese post offices and consulates were opened in the main treaty ports. Japanese merchants came in by the hundreds, and Japanese teachers were to be found in Chinese government schools. Since 1901 Chinese students had flocked to Japan by the thousands, finding in Tokyo a nearer and less expensive source of Western learning than the university centers of the West. Returning, they had given a decidedly Japanese flavor to the reform movement in their home land.

The Chinese revolution of 1911 that overthrew the Manchu dynasty and established in its place a republic gave Japan fresh opportunities for interference in the internal affairs of her neighbor. It is true that the revolution was accompanied by a patriotic movement that resented foreign influence, but with the revolution came disorder and temporary decentralization. The one led to offenses against a few individual Japanese, which gave Tokyo an opportunity to overawe the Chinese by vigorous demands for satisfaction. The other weakened Peking. It has not been proved that the Tokyo government ever gave Chinese rebels direct aid, but individual, over-enthusiastic Japanese, some of them officials, were guilty of helping them. The revolution, too, brought a need for more money to pay troops and to maintain and reorganize the government. A group of foreign bankers, made up originally of representatives of France, Germany, England, and the United States, offered to make a huge loan to be secured by receipts from taxes, notably the salt monopoly, and on the condition that in the future China should borrow exclusively from that group. Japan and Russia demanded and obtained entrance into the charmed circle, and the "sextuple syndicate" seemed about to institute a joint protectorate over China's finances. The American members of the syndicate withdrew soon after President Wilson came into office, for he had declined his support on the ground that by the terms of the loan China's autonomy would be jeopardized. The representatives of the remaining five powers made the loan, although this did not carry with it quite the drastic monopoly on the finances of China that had at first been contemplated. Japan, with the other four powers, was by it given a firmer hold on China.

RELATIONS WITH CHINA, 1914–1916

Then in August, 1914, came the first World War. By the terms of her alliance with Great Britain, Japan was under obligation to come to the former's assistance in case she were attacked in the Far East, and to consider in common with her the measures that should be taken to safeguard any interests in the same region that were threatened by the Germans. Japan was quite ready to assume to the full her obligations under the alliance, for it gave her an opportunity to establish herself in China and the Pacific. With the European powers busy elsewhere and with the reluctance of the United States to use force to preserve the open door, she could do on the neighboring continent almost as she pleased. On August 15th Japan presented a note to the German government "advising" it to withdraw from Far Eastern waters all its men-of-war and armed vessels, to disarm those that could not be withdrawn, and to give up to her the leased territory of Kiaochow "with a view to the eventual restoration of the same to China." The note reminded one of the German communication to Japan in 1895.

Germany sent no reply and Japan entered the war. She aided England in clearing Asiatic waters of German cruisers and raiders and captured some of the German Pacific islands which later became of such strategic importance. With some slight assistance from her ally she sent a force to China and after a siege captured Tsingtao and occupied the German railways and mines in Shantung. Count Okuma, then the premier, publicly and in writing disavowed Japanese territorial ambitions. Japan said she had "no ulterior motive, no desire to secure more territory, no thought of depriving China or other peoples of anything which they now possess." The temptation offered by the unusual opportunity, however, proved very great, too great, in fact, to be entirely resisted. In the attack on Tsingtao China's neutrality was not respected and repeated complaints were made by the Chinese of usurpations of authority by Japanese troops and officials in and near the railway zone. Tsingtao was treated as conquered territory, even to the exclusion of British interests.

But Japan was preparing for a more far-reaching move. Early in 1915 she made demands on Peking, demands which if granted in full would place the huge continental republic completely under the power of Japan. These "Twenty-One Demands," as they were known, fell into five groups.

First: in regard to Shantung, China was to promise to give her assent to anything upon which the Japanese and German governments might agree in regard to the rights which the latter possessed in the province. She was to engage not to cede or to lease to any third power any territory within or along the coast of Shantung. She was to give to Japan an additional railway concession and to open new ports to trade.

Second: in regard to South Manchuria and Eastern Inner Mongolia, the leases on the railways and ports held by Japan were to be extended to ninety-nine years instead of the twenty-five years for which they were first made. Japanese officials and civilians were to have the right not only in the railway zones and treaty ports, but everywhere in the two regions, to travel, to reside, to lease or buy land for trading, manufacturing or agricultural purposes, to engage in any business they wished, and to open such mines as China and Japan might agree upon. Such extensive privileges of residence and ownership of land had not been granted elsewhere in China to foreigners other than missionaries: extraterritorial rights required the restriction of most foreign residence and business to treaty ports, where the necessary consular courts could be operated without too much prejudice to Chinese jurisdiction. China was to promise, too, that the Japanese government would be consulted before any foreign advisers were employed for South Manchuria or Eastern Inner Mongolia and that before Peking granted a railway concession or made a loan on the security of the taxes of these districts, Tokyo's consent would first be obtained. A lease was to be given Japan on a short railway hitherto outside its control. The effect of this second group of concessions, if they were granted, would be to strengthen Japan's control over some of the richest sections of China to the exclusion of all possible interference from the outside, while still preserving the semblance of the open door and Chinese sovereignty.

Third: the Han-yeh-ping Company, a home-owned enterprise which operated the greatest iron works in China, and which controlled extensive bodies of iron ore and coal, was to be made the joint undertaking of Japan and China. Without the consent of the former the latter was not to dispose of her rights in the company, and without the company's permission she was not to permit mines in the neighborhood of those owned by it to be worked, or any enterprise affecting its interests to be undertaken. The properties of the Han-yeh-ping Company were in the heart of China, within the region that less than twenty years before had been marked out by the British as a sphere of influence. The company was in financial straits and had already borrowed from Japanese. Its control by the Japanese and the strengthening of their political influence in that region would be made certain were the demand granted. Japan, sadly deficient in iron ore of her own, would be assured a supply that would probably be adequate for years to come.

Fourth: China was not to cede or to lease to any other power than Japan any harbor, bay, or island along her coast.

The fifth group comprised a series of demands which more completely than the other four would, if granted, place China under the control of her neighbor. The Chinese government was to employ Japanese as advisers in political, financial, and military affairs; the police departments of important places in China were to be under the joint administration of the two nations; China was either to purchase of her neighbor fifty per cent or more of her munitions of

such vigor that their commerce in China, their most vulnerable point, suffered greatly. Public opinion in China was such that all the attempts made by Japan in the following two years for some compromise of the Shantung controversy

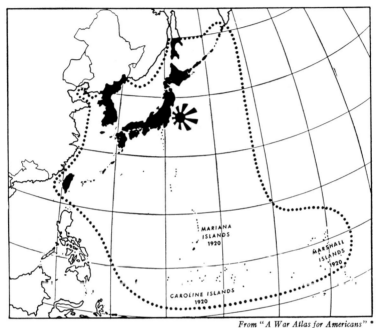

From "A War Atlas for Americans" *

Peace conference haul, Treaty of Versailles, 1919

were rejected. In 1920 the pro-Japanese clique was driven out of power. In spite of her political helplessness, China was developing a spirit which boded ill for Japan and which led Tokyo to doubt the wisdom of the Continental policy that since 1914 had seemed so effective.

JAPAN IN SIBERIA, 1918–1925

After the collapse of the Russian imperial government, in 1917, the Czecho-Slovaks who had been held as prisoners

* Prepared with the assistance of the Office of War Information. Published by Simon and Schuster.

of war in Siberia attempted to get back to Europe to join the Allied armies. Their only available route was by way of Eastern Siberia and the Pacific, but as disorder in Siberia increased, their safety was threatened. There was, accordingly, sent to Siberia in 1918 an allied expedition, the largest group being from Japan and the next largest from the United States. The Japanese sent a much larger force than the United States Government had been led to expect, and fear was expressed that in the general disorder Japan would find a reason for keeping her troops on the continent after the original purpose of the expedition had been effected. The frontiers of Korea seemed in danger, there were many Japanese residents in Siberia, and there were involved relations with the governments which came into existence in Siberia. A further complication was added when, in 1920, at Nikolaievsk, on the Amur River, opposite Karafuto, several hundred Japanese, including the consul, were murdered by a guerrilla band which expressed sympathy with the Russian Bolshevist régime.

However, the last of the Czecho-Slovak troops left Vladivostok on their way home in September, 1920. In January, 1920, the American government had decided to withdraw its forces. Great Britain, France and Italy removed their troops, and Japan began to call home her army. Although for some time Japan maintained garrisons in Vladivostok and the vicinity and in Northern Manchuria, by the end of 1922 these had been removed. Giving the Nikolaievsk incident as the reason, however, the Japanese Government still occupied the Russian half of Karafuto. Various conferences between the Japanese and the Soviet authorities followed. Three of these proved fruitless of permanent results, but early in 1925 a treaty was signed whereby diplomatic relations between the two countries were restored and the Japanese army was withdrawn from the occupied territory. Certain concessions for coal and mineral oil in Northern Karafuto were, however, granted to the Japanese. The entire Siberian expedition had been a costly one, both in money and in the suspicion and ill-will of other powers. Japan had gotten from it little glory and much anxiety.

JAPAN AT THE PARIS PEACE CONFERENCE AND IN THE TREATY OF VERSAILLES, 1919

As one of the more important participants in the first World War, Japan naturally had a prominent place at the Peace Conference. Her delegation, however, confined its attention chiefly to securing Japan's interests in the Far East and the Pacific. To Japan's demand for racial equality the Conference turned a deaf ear, but much more tangible gains were accorded, the possession of the German properties in Shantung, a mandate (under the League of Nations) over the former German islands in the Pacific north of the Equator — the Mariana (Ladrone), Caroline, and Marshall groups — and one of the five permanent seats in the Council of the League of Nations. Japan had at last been formally recognized as one of the major world powers.

RELATIONS BETWEEN THE UNITED STATES AND JAPAN, 1894–1921

During the years since 1894 Japan's relations with the United States had been undergoing a change. From the time of the Perry expedition the two countries had had for many years the most cordial attitude toward each other. The United States had never been suspected of territorial ambitions in the Far East. She had repeatedly by acts of generosity demonstrated the cordiality of her friendship for her trans-Pacific neighbor. She looked with a kind of benevolent pride upon Japan's rapid development, and saw in it no menace to her own safety. The two nations coöperated in seeking to maintain the open door in Manchuria after the Boxer uprising. In the war with Russia American sympathies were all with the Japanese; New York bankers loaned a large proportion of the funds needed for the struggle, and President Theodore Roosevelt went about as far as was possible for an American chief executive in assuring Japan of the support of his government. In return Japan looked upon America as the one great Western power from whom she had nothing to fear and was moved by gratitude for the evidences of disinterested friendship that had been shown her. Many Japanese students found their way to American universities and took back with them a hearty admiration for the country where they had spent their college days. The United States, moreover, had provided Japan a market for tea and raw silk, especially the latter, and was her best customer, better even than China. In return Japan bought from the United States large quantities of raw cotton, manufactures, machinery, iron, and steel.

By the close of 1905, however, friction between the two countries began to develop. A portion of the Japanese public was inclined to regard the United States as responsible for the terms of the unpopular Treaty of Portsmouth which ended the war with Russia. This slight resentment would quickly have died out had there not soon been added other causes for trouble. The first of these was the immigration question. The Pacific Coast states of America were poorly supplied with the cheap labor needed for their development. Chinese unskilled labor had been excluded by Congress and the newer European immigrants did not quickly find their way across the country. Unskilled Japanese workmen, then, found an open field on our west coast, at wages far greater than what they could hope for at home. Many Japanese came to the Pacific Coast and especially to California and were accompanied or followed by a few merchants and professional men. Immigration grew when the United States annexed Hawaii. Tens of thousands of Japanese had come to the islands during the years of independence to work on the plantations. After 1898 they began to go to America. This influx of cheap Asiatic labor alarmed the people of the west coast. The Japanese, it was felt, could not be assimilated easily if at all. Their home country was known to be crowded by a rapidly growing population, and it was feared that unless their immigration were stopped they would soon form a large un-American group on the thinly settled Pacific Coast. White laborers would be unable or unwilling to compete with a race whose standards of living were so much lower than their own and would either become poverty-stricken or withdraw; the coast states would be filled with an ever increasing Oriental population and might in time become a Japanese rather than an American community. These fears were to some extent justified. Some Americans felt a strong prejudice against the Japanese. With such a prejudice, friction was inevitable, intermarriage was frowned upon, and assimilation made difficult. As early as 1900 there had been some trouble, and the Tokyo government, to avoid friction, had passed restrictions on emigration to the United States. In 1903 a labor convention in Chicago appointed a commission to study the question and the report was opposed to Japanese immigration. In 1905 a league to exclude Japanese and Koreans was organized in San Francisco, and in 1906 the question came to a head when the San Francisco school officials attempted to segregate the Japanese from the American pupils. At President Theodore Roosevelt's suggestion the local authorities agreed to drop the matter, but only on the condition that the federal government would undertake to put a stop to further immigration of Japanese from Hawaii, Mexico, and Canada. Congress in 1907 passed an act authorizing the president to prevent further immigration of the Japanese. The president then by proclamation prohibited the movement from Hawaii, Mexico, and Canada. He also entered into negotiations with Tokyo which led to the so-called "Gentlemen's Agreement" by which Japan agreed to prevent any of her laboring class from coming to America.

In 1913 friction again arose over legislation in California, when, in spite of President Woodrow Wilson's representations through Secretary of State Bryan, a bill was passed which forbade Japanese to hold agricultural land in the state except on a short-term lease. Similar legislation was talked of in Oregon and Idaho in 1917 and was withdrawn only on requests from Washington. Naturalization has not been allowed, and only American-born Japanese have or can acquire the rights of citizenship. The Japanese people were offended by this American legislation, partly because of the scant respect for their feelings that had been shown in discussing and enacting it, and partly because it seemed to them unwarranted discrimination.

Another source of friction between Japan and the United States was the conflict of interests of the two powers in the Far East. In 1898 America acquired the Philippines and in the same year annexed Hawaii. This, from the American standpoint, was the unavoidable result of the force of circumstances. From the Japanese standpoint it seemed as if America had designs on China. Shortly afterward, as if to confirm Japan's worst suspicions, the United States began to champion the principle of the open door in China, a principle which after 1905 threatened the special interests acquired by Japan in Manchuria through the Treaty of Portsmouth. American capitalists attempted to get from China concessions for a railway which would have competed with the Japanese roads in Manchuria, and were prevented only by the opposition of Tokyo. Still later came the Knox proposal to purchase and operate these same Japanese Manchurian roads by an international syndicate. This from the standpoint of Americans was designed merely to preserve the open door and Chinese independence, but to Japan it seemed to be actuated by purely selfish motives and to threaten the fruits of her dearly won victories.

Still later Americans began to invest capital in China. American bankers joined in the six-power loan to China until discouraged by President Wilson. The Standard Oil Company obtained a partial monopoly on the oil fields of China, although that was later surrendered, and an American company entered into negotiations to build great docks in Fukien province, opposite the Japanese-owned Formosa. In 1916 other American capitalists proposed a loan for railway construction that competed with Japanese interests in Shantung. American sentiment had been vigorously opposed to Japanese aggressions in China during the first World War, and it was due largely to pressure from the United States that China in 1917 broke with Germany. The United States had had an important part in the Allied expedition to Siberia in 1918–1920 and at the Paris Conference had been the chief opponent to Japan's claim to the former German possessions in Shantung. Americans had in 1920 led to the formation of a new financial organization for the control of foreign loans to China, and Japan had been given membership in it only when she had withdrawn her objections to including Manchuria and Eastern Inner Mongolia within its scope.

All of this seemed very reasonable and just to the average citizen of the United States. He was innocent of any imperialistic intentions in Asia and wanted only an open door of equal opportunity. To some Japanese minds, however, there was a sinister aspect to this American westward expansion. In the course of a hundred years or so the United States had jumped the Mississippi River, crossed the Rockies, occupied the Pacific slope, and since Japan's war with China had spanned the Pacific, acquiring Hawaii and the Philippines, was seeking investments in Chinese mines and railways, and was interfering in Far Eastern politics. What might she not do next?

Many Americans were suspicious of Japan's designs in the Far East and the Pacific. They feared that she was only waiting her opportunity to seize the Philippines and Hawaii and even portions of the American Continent. They pointed to the large Japanese elements in the Hawaiian Islands as a source of danger, and listened to rumors of Japanese political designs on Mexico, and Central and South America. They viewed with alarm the growth of Japanese shipping on the Pacific which was rapidly increasing while American shipping on the same waters was declining.

Friction between the United States and Japan over China was partly allayed for the time by an exchange of notes which grew out of the visit to America in the summer and autumn of 1917 of a Japanese commission headed by Viscount Ishii. The United States frankly recognized "That territorial propinquity creates special relations between countries . . . [and] that Japan has special interests in China, particularly in that part to which her possessions are contiguous." She expressed her faith that Japan would observe the open door and the territorial integrity and independence of China. To this Japan readily agreed, and declared with the United States, that she was "opposed to the acquisition by any government of any special rights or privileges that would affect the independence or territorial integrity of China or that would deny to the subjects or citizens of any country the full enjoyment of equal opportunity in the commerce and industry of China." The agreement was greeted with no great enthusiasm by the press in either America or

Japan, for to many of the public in both countries it seemed that each foreign office had conceded too much. The Chinese were bitter in their denunciation. The agreement seemed to them to be the desertion of their last remaining protector against the aggressions of Japan, and Peking registered a formal refusal to be bound by any conventions to which she was not a willing party.

The Lansing-Ishii Agreement was not an adequate adjustment of the differences between Japan and the United States, and the closing years of World War I, the Paris Conference, and the years immediately following the Treaty of Versailles saw other and grave causes for friction added to those which already troubled the peace between the two powers. The Siberian expedition aroused jealousies and suspicions on both sides; among the Japanese, because they resented active American intervention in Asiatic regions so close to Japan, among Americans, because they believed that the Japanese military authorities had not kept faith and were seeking to make the expedition a step toward the permanent occupation of part of Siberia. The award to Japan by the Treaty of Versailles of the former German holdings in Shantung was loudly denounced by most Americans as one of the most objectionable features of that unpopular document and the criticism could scarcely be received calmly by the Japanese.

The American government objected to the occupation by Japan of the Island of Yap, an important cable center in the Pacific, and one of the Caroline group which had been awarded her at Paris under mandate to the League of Nations, claiming that specific reservations about it had been made by President Wilson and that it should be internationalized. A reported American concession in Siberia aroused resentment in Japan, and the remnant of Japanese good-will was threatened by expanding American trade in China, an American wireless contract with the Chinese Government, and the new American-led organization for the financing of China. Competition in naval construction spread further the rapidly increasing friction. In both countries there were many who believed that war was inevitable and imminent. The British authorities were concerned, for the Anglo-Japanese Alliance might embroil not only Great Britain but Canada and Australia in the impending war and lead to strain within the British Empire. It was obvious that some peaceable adjustment of existing difficulties must be sought and sought quickly.

THE WASHINGTON CONFERENCE, 1921–1922

To prevent the threatened conflict between the United States and Japan and other wars which were looming because of the clash of rival policies in the Pacific and the increase of naval armaments, the United States Government called an international conference. This met in Washington in the winter of 1921–1922 and at it were represented the British Empire, France, Japan, China, Belgium, Italy, the Netherlands, Portugal, and the United States. The Conference, for a time, cleared many of the existing causes of friction, not only between Japan and the United States but between Japan and China. One treaty was negotiated which limited naval armaments and forbade the construction of additional fortifications in certain Pacific islands. By the "Four Power Treaty" the United States, the British Empire, France, and Japan agreed to call joint conferences to adjust future controversies over their island possessions in the Pacific, if such controversies could not be settled by diplomacy, and promised to respect each other's rights in these possessions. The treaty also provided for the ending of the Anglo-Japanese Alliance. The Nine Power Pact renewed and expressed the international promise to respect the sovereignty and territorial integrity of China and the principles of the Open Door. Still another treaty promised an adjustment of the Chinese tariff. There were various resolutions which had as their object the reduction of foreign control over China's autonomy and the publication of treaties, conventions, and the like which affected China. Japan and China took the opportunity to adjust their differences over Shantung. Japan's holdings in Shantung were conveyed to the Chinese on terms which were on the whole satisfactory to both parties. Japan and the United States, too, effected a compromise of their difficulties over the Island of Yap. The occasion for the Lansing-Ishii Agreement having passed, that document was annulled on March 30, 1923. As a result of the Washington Conference the danger of war in the Pacific seemed greatly lessened. Not all Japanese and Americans were satisfied with the adjustment. Some of the former believed that too much had been conceded, and some of the latter pointed to the undoubted fact that as long as the treaties were observed Japan was assured of the military and naval control of the northeastern coast of Asia. For the time being, however, the voices of discord were almost silenced.

RELATIONS BETWEEN THE UNITED STATES AND JAPAN, 1922–1931

The happier relations established by the Washington Conference continued for several years. The seeming observance by Japan of her obligations under the Washington treaties and the adoption of a milder policy in China and Korea lessened American criticism, and the prompt and substantial aid given by citizens of the United States at the time of the disastrous earthquake in Japan in September, 1923, aroused gratitude in the hearts of many Japanese.

In 1924, however, the new general immigration law replaced the "Gentlemen's Agreement." This reawakened feeling against the United States in Japan. This new law prohibited the entrance of "all aliens ineligible to citizenship" (and this included the Japanese) except government officials, merchants, and tourists in this country "temporarily," immigrants returning from a visit abroad, ministers and professors and their wives and children under eighteen, and *bona fide* students at least fifteen years of age. This act in fact canceled the "Gentlemen's Agreement," the United States now, rather than Japan, prohibiting immigration and enforcing that prohibition, and on a slightly stricter basis.

The act gave great offense in Japan, partly because of its substance and its discrimination, for it seemed to imply that the Japanese along with other Asiatics are inferior. To the Japanese the measure seemed an insult. Proponents of the bill contended, however, that the admission of aliens to the United States was a purely domestic matter and should not be subject to the consent of a foreign power; that Japanese were not necessarily inferior but because of their Oriental background were less able to assimilate than Europeans, and that Japan had seemed to be trying to threaten America into admitting her subjects. To the Japanese these reasons seemed inadequate and there was both indignation and a sense of deep injury. There were few acts against Americans in Japan, for the Government was prompt to discourage and suppress mob violence, but it was obvious to all observers that relations between the two powers had been subjected to a strain which time might increase rather than remove. This strain was increased by the desire of Japan to control affairs in China and by the United States' support of the Open Door.

RELATIONS BETWEEN CHINA AND JAPAN, 1922–1931

Beginning with the Washington Conference, the Japanese Government adopted a much more conciliatory attitude toward China. The country was experiencing a more moderate government and consequently pursuing a softer policy abroad. The Shantung properties were returned in strict accordance with the agreement made at Washington, and Japan's post-offices in the country were closed by the date specified in the Washington agreements. Violence against individual Japanese and even against the flag was not followed by such demands as before 1922. Although Japan was less aggressive than during and after the first World War, her interest in China was no less keen and she was by no means disposed to relinquish further her holdings in the country. She was speedily developing her leaseholds in Manchuria. While, in common with most of the powers, Japan remitted the unpaid portion of the Boxer indemnity due her, she, like some others of them, arranged to have it allocated to objects which would at least do her no harm and which might possibly increase her influence in China. In May, 1925, trouble broke out in Shanghai over a strike in a Japanese-owned mill. On May 30th student sympathizers with the strikers were shot down by the police in the International Settlement while demonstrating in favor of the laborers. The wave of indignation which followed swept rapidly over the nation and led among other things to a boycott against both British and Japanese. The Japanese did not, however, suffer as greatly as did the British nor did they retaliate vigorously.

When, in March, 1927, the Chinese Nationalist forces took Nanking, foreigners were very roughly handled. Japanese suffered with the others. The Japanese consulate was looted and some Japanese, including the consul, were wounded. The Japanese government, however, contented itself with joining four of the other aggrieved powers in a demand for the punishment of the commanders of the guilty troops, an apology, and reparation for injuries and damages. In April,

1927, Japanese were attacked and injured in the Japanese concession at Hankow, but still Tokyo showed much restraint. In the summer of 1927, as the northward advance of the Nationalists continued, Japan dispatched troops to Shantung, where there were many Japanese residents, saying that she wished to prevent there a recurrence of what had happened to her citizens in Nanking and Hankow. She withdrew them in the autumn when the Nationalist tide receded. In 1928, however, when the Nationalists once more advanced, she again sent troops to Shantung, for hundreds of Japanese civilians were still there. When, in May, 1928, the Nationalists reached Tsinan, the capital of Shantung, Japanese and Chinese forces clashed, there was loss of life on both sides, and each accused the other of outrages. For a time the Japanese were left in control of the city, a vigorous anti-Japanese boycott once more swept over China, and the relations between the two countries were greatly strained. The following March, Japan reached an agreement with the Chinese (Nationalist) Government, and in May, 1929, the Japanese forces were once more withdrawn from the province.

As nationalist sentiment mounted in China, Japan's position in Manchuria continued to prove an irritation. More than ever, Japan felt that she could not retire. Her capital investments were growing, and the coal and iron resources of the region, especially the iron, were important for her industries. The Chinese were attempting to build a railway system of their own in Manchuria to make them in part independent of the Japanese roads, and as an outlet for it were developing a port at Hulutao. Fortunately the government maintained in Manchuria by the Chinese under Chang Tsolin was much more nearly stable than that which existed in much of the rest of China, there was less disorder and consequently less danger to Japanese lives and property, and no such serious armed clashes occurred as that in Shantung. In June, 1928, Chang Tso-lin was fatally wounded by a bomb as he was retreating to Mukden before the Nationalists, and it was widely believed that Japanese were responsible. The charge, indeed, later caused a serious crisis in the Japanese Diet. However, although Chang Tso-lin was succeeded by his son, Chang Hsüeh-liang, and the latter affiliated himself with the Nationalists, no break occurred with Japan. Japan insisted that her primary interests in Manchuria were economic, not political, and in spite of denunciations by Chinese Nationalists, did not wish to make an issue at that time. It seemed clear, however, that Manchuria remained a danger spot.

The growing movement in China for the recovery of tariff autonomy and the abolition of extraterritoriality was a cause of grave concern to Japan. Her trade with China was a considerable percentage of her foreign commerce. An increase of Chinese import duties was a more serious matter for her than for the United States or Great Britain, who with her had the largest shares of China's maritime commerce. Therefore, when China asked for tariff revision and suggested that it be on the basis of "equality and reciprocity," the Japanese opposed her efforts. When, however, Great Britain, the United States, and a number of the other powers consented to China's resumption of tariff autonomy, and, on February 1, 1929, this came into effect, Japan at the last moment gave in. However, Japan did not consent to the abolition of extraterritoriality.

JAPAN AND WORLD PEACE, 1922–1931

As we have seen, the Washington Conference by relieving the tension between Japan and the United States, regulating the size of navies, and adjusting the situation in the Pacific in a manner fairly satisfactory to the Japanese, marked an epoch in Japan's foreign policies. She had nothing immediately to fear from Western sea powers, and as a permanent member of the Council of the League of Nations she had an assured and honorable position in international society. At the Arms Conference in London in 1930 Japan requested a ratio in naval strength which was somewhat greater than that allowed at Washington and which would have meant a marked increase in expenditures. Moreover, she was building warships of types not restricted by the treaty despite the fact that her action violated the spirit of the treaty. However, in spite of the protests of some of her naval men, she accepted a compromise which involved a substantial reduction from her first demands.

Japan, moreover, had been one of the signers (1928) to the Pact of Paris for "the renunciation of war as an instrument of national policy." Her official ratification was delayed for some time, but finally was completed. The liberals in charge of the government were able to overcome the opposition of the Nationalists, but the acceptance of the London agreement was a challenge to the basic position of the militarists. They met this challenge with the arguments of self-interest and patriotism to make a case against the "weak" foreign policy. These arguments, inspired by Army leaders, were spread by numerous patriotic societies.

FRESH JAPANESE EXPANSION IN ASIA:
THE ESTABLISHMENT OF MANCHUKUO

The peaceful temper which in the early part of 1931 seemed to characterize Japanese foreign policy was suddenly interrupted. In the summer and autumn of 1931 a conflict arose in Manchuria which led to the extension of Japan's control on the continent and which brought severe strain upon Japan's relations with most of the Western nations.

As we have seen, the rising tide of Chinese nationalism

sought to curb Russia and Japan in Manchuria. Recurrent friction between the powers represented in that area was inevitable. Sooner or later all but one would be compelled to retire. In 1929 China had attempted, unsuccessfully, further to restrict the Russians. By competing railways and a new port the Chinese were building a transportation system which would make them independent of the Japanese South Manchuria Railroad and Dairen. To this the Japanese objected.

In the summer of 1931 clashes occurred in Manchuria and Korea between Chinese and Koreans (the latter being Japanese subjects).

Suddenly, in September, 1931, the Japanese struck. An explosion on the South Manchuria Railroad near Mukden was the signal. Within a few weeks the forces of Chang Hsüeh-liang were eliminated from Manchuria. Instead of his rule the Japanese encouraged local authorities to form governments under their protection. In the spring of 1932 a régime was set up, under the name of Manchukuo, for the entire region. To its head was called the last Manchu Emperor of China, Pu-yi. In 1934 the new state assumed the title of an empire. A close alliance was formed with Japan, and Japanese advisers were prominent in the administration. Policy was directed by the commander-in-chief of the Kwantung Army in his capacity as Japanese ambassador to Manchukuo.

China did not tamely submit to the loss of Manchuria. She took her case to the League of Nations. That body was in an embarrassing position, for in the Far East it would need to depend chiefly upon Great Britain for the enforcement of its decisions. Great Britain was reluctant to act in any manner which might bring her into war with Japan. Eventually a commission was appointed, under the chairmanship of Lord Lytton, to investigate and make recommendations. The commission, in general, reported Japan to be at fault and recommended a method of settlement which the Japanese were unwilling to accept. The negotiations dragged on for months, and ended in 1933, in the withdrawal of Japan from the League.

In the meantime, in January, 1932, hostilities broke out between Japanese and Chinese in Shanghai. In the ensuing struggle, part of the city was destroyed. The Chinese offered a more stubborn resistance than had been anticipated, but in time were driven back. Not for several months did a Chinese-Japanese agreement end the trouble.

Although not a member of the League of Nations, the United States was deeply concerned in the Manchurian incident, for she was involved through several treaties, including the nine power document of 1922 and the Pact of Paris. For a time she coöperated with the League. In January, 1932, she came out independently, although not without previous consultation with Great Britain, France, and Italy, with what was known, after the name of her Secretary of State (later Secretary of War) who formulated it, as the Stimson doctrine. By this the United States declined to recognize any agreement concluded by China and Japan which would impair her treaty rights, "including those which relate to the sovereignty, independence, territorial and administrative integrity of the Republic of China" or any situation, treaty, or agreement made contrary to the treaties and obligations of the Pact of Paris.

Both the members of the League and the United States declined to give Manchukuo official recognition. Only tardily, by 1938, did a few nations do so — Salvador first, then Germany and Italy.

However, Japan was undaunted. In 1935, after months of negotiation, Manchukuo, through the good offices of Tokyo, purchased the Russian interest in the Chinese Eastern Railroad. This left Japan the sole foreign power with an effective voice or holdings in the new state.

Japan set about the development of Manchukuo for her own profit. She poured in vast sums of capital. She built railways. She sought, though with disappointingly slight

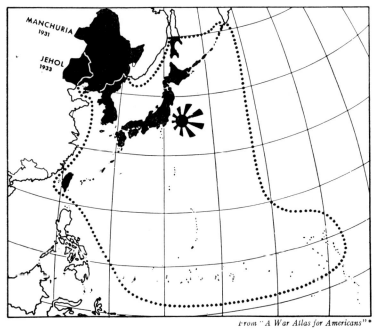

From "A War Atlas for Americans"*

The doorway to Asia, 1931–33

success, to encourage extensive Japanese immigration. Within a few years, however, it became obvious that her dreams of quick relief for her economic problems through Manchukuo were not to be fulfilled. Indeed, it was an open question whether the Manchukuoan adventure was not to be a liability rather than an asset. The enmity of much of the rest of the world and the cost of maintaining and defending the new state were only partially offset by

* Prepared with the assistance of the Office of War Information. Published by Simon and Schuster.

gains in markets and raw materials. Much of the population of Manchukuo remained unreconciled to the new régime. The Japanese felt themselves compelled to take drastic measures to suppress what they called "banditry." Much of the farming population was forcibly concentrated in villages which the Japanese could so control that the "bandits" might be segregated and starved out. The cost of policing the country was great.

THE BREAKDOWN OF ATTEMPTS AT NAVAL DISARMAMENT

The relations between Japan on the one hand and Great Britain and the United States on the other, already strained by the creation of Manchukuo, were made worse by unsuccessful attempts to prevent competition in naval armaments. To be sure, the naval conference at London in 1930 had extended until 1936 the holiday in the building of capital ships. However, the Japanese were unhappy over the apparently subordinate position given them by the Washington Conference. That Conference had fixed the ratio in capital ship tonnage between the principal navies, those of Great Britain, the United States, and Japan, at 5-5-3. While this assured Japan a strong maritime position in the Far East, by limiting her to a smaller navy than those of the two others it appeared to her to be unfair. She insisted, therefore, upon the principle of equality. In 1934 conversations on naval questions were resumed by the powers, but with an unsatisfactory outcome. In December, 1934, Japan served notice that, at the end of 1936, she would cease to be bound by the limitations which she had accepted in 1922. All three powers soon began increasing their navies and a new era of competition began. This was increased, in 1938, by the adoption by the United States of an enlarged program of building and by the refusal of Japan to deny that she was designing capital ships of an unusually large size.

JAPAN IN THE COMPETITION FOR WORLD TRADE

In the nineteen thirties Japan became an increasingly formidable competitor of the West in the markets of the world. Her low labor costs, her depreciation of the yen, and

By Ewing Galloway, N.Y.

Japanese bicycles made for export sold more cheaply than those of any other country. Labor costs were low.

the reorganization of some of her industries enabled her to sell many of her manufactures at prices far below those which Western producers could meet. The world-wide economic depression which came after 1929 led in many countries to a demand for cheap goods. The volume of Japanese exports greatly increased. In India Japanese cottons partly displaced native and British textiles. The Dutch East Indies were flooded with Japanese goods. Japanese merchants increased their sales in Latin America. Even in the United States and Western Europe some Japanese products cut into the markets of domestic manufacturers. In several countries irritation against the Japanese became acute. In many lands in one manner or another restrictions were placed on Japanese imports. The one outlet which Japan had left to relieve her difficult economic situation seemed blocked. Because of the opposition of Western peoples extensive emigration had long been impossible. Now the sale of the products of Japan's factories was threatened.

CONTINUED JAPANESE EXPANSION AT THE EXPENSE OF CHINA

The formation of Manchukuo was the forerunner of the further extension of Japanese control on the continent at the expense of China.

The Japanese military authorities felt it necessary to round out Manchukuo by the annexation of the province of Jehol, the easternmost portion of Inner Mongolia. This was accomplished by force of arms in 1933. In May, 1933, the Tangku Truce was signed with China. By this a demilitarized zone was created along the eastern portion of the Great Wall and Chinese troops in the region were replaced by a Chinese police force.

Japan was not content with this. Late in 1935 an area in the eastern part of Hopei, the province which embraced Tientsin and Peking, was separated from Nationalist China by the formation of the East Hopei Autonomous Council, made up of Chinese under the thinly veiled domination of the Japanese military authorities.

Much of the rest of Hopei, plus the province of Chahar, in Inner Mongolia, was partially abstracted from Nationalist China by the creation of a Hopei-Chahar Military Council.

This, however, was not so much under Japanese control as was the régime in Eastern Hopei.

Through this Japanese-controlled area in North-east China extensive smuggling of Japanese goods took place into Nationalist China, to the annoyance and loss of the latter.

Japan's maritime service unloading food supplies from a transport steamer

Much criticism was voiced, too, over the extensive sale of narcotics in the North-eastern region by Japanese subjects, both Koreans and Japanese.

Japan was fearful of Russia. Her military leaders believed a war with Russia to be all but inevitable. Repeated clashes occurred along the Amur and on the border between Manchoukuo and the Russian-protected Outer Mongolia. Friction occurred, too, over fishing rights in the waters off Eastern Siberia. The Japanese developed a hatred for communism and professed to fear it. In November, 1936, the Japanese Government entered into an anti-communist pact with Nazi Germany. In 1937 Japan and Fascist Italy reached an agreement against communism. This is usually called the anti-Comintern Pact.

Japan continued to press China. She urged the Nationalist Government to join her in economic coöperation and in stamping out communism in China. It happened that the Chinese Government was engaged in a campaign to crush the communist opposition, but it feared that coöperation with Japan would mean actually not coöperation but subordination.

Japan was increasingly emphatic that she had special interests in China and would not brook the efforts of any other nation or of the League to strengthen China against her, or the attempt of China to seek the aid of other powers. In April, 1934, indeed, the spokesman of the Foreign Office in Tokyo came out pointedly with a pronouncement to this effect.

It was clear, moreover, that the Japanese were endeavoring to draw all of Inner Mongolia and North-eastern China within their control and there to set up local governments which they could control. The provinces of Chahar, Suiyüan, Hopei, Shantung, Shansi, and Shensi were included in this program. From the military standpoint the purpose was to seek safeguards against an attack from Russia and against Russian overland aid to China. From the financial standpoint, the rich natural resources of the area would prove profitable for Japanese capitalists and so relieve some of the economic pressure in Japan.

This Japanese expansion aroused the bitter enmity of the Chinese. Anti-Japanese boycotts were invoked against

Japanese trade. After 1931 the Chinese more and more believed war with Japan the only alternative to absorption by their island neighbor. Under the pressure of the common danger the political unification of China was hastened. Late in 1936 even the antagonism between the Nationalist Government at Nanking, led by Chiang Kai-shek, and the Chinese communists was forgotten in meeting the Japanese menace. For in 1936 Japan appeared a menace not only to the Chinese but to other Pacific powers as well. With few exceptions the militarists were becoming increasingly the dominant factor in Japanese politics and were taking matters into their own hands. Their policy reflected the attitude of the intensely nationalistic groups in Japan who gradually committed the nation to war.

CHAPTER XII

The Internal Development of Japan from the War with China to VJ Day (1894–1945)

The half century which succeeded the Chino-Japanese war of 1894–1895 was marked by important and striking developments within Japan. These were not as spectacular as those of the preceding forty years. Nor did they attract as much attention from the world at large either as the changes which followed the advent of Commodore Perry or as the acquisition of foreign territory by Japan in the half century after 1894. They were, however, quite as important as either of these. They were less revolutionary than the alterations set in motion by the coming of Perry. They were not as startling as the overseas conquests of the Empire. Yet in large part they accounted for the latter. Japan's imperial ambitions and her phenomenal territorial expansion cannot be understood apart from the internal life of the land in these fateful five decades.

The alterations in Japan in the generation or so after 1894 were chiefly a continuation of those in the preceding forty years. Basically Japanese culture was less in a state of change than was the civilization of China during those same eventful decades. It was characteristic of the revolution in Japan that it was directed from the top and was accomplished with smaller disturbance to the established structure and ideals of the nation than would have seemed possible if one gave attention merely to the superficial aspects. The imperial institution was perpetuated and even strengthened, some of the ancient families, including the Fujiwara and the Tokugawa, remained prominent, loyalty to Japan as personified in the emperor was, if anything, heightened, and the fundamental social unit, the family, was conserved. Yet Japan could not be in the world of the twentieth century without showing the effects. That world was one in which Western civilization was continuing to impinge upon non-Western peoples and with increasing power. Everywhere it was working changes. Moreover, Western culture was itself undergoing profound and rapid transformation. Non-European peoples were, accordingly, experiencing a double revolution: one was that which came from the penetration of Western culture and the other was that which issued from the fact that this culture was itself in process of revolution.

The changes which most caught the eye were in the realms of economics, government, and social structure. Those in thought and ideology were less immediately spectacular, but they were important and must also be noted if we are to understand Japan. It is to a description of these alterations that we now turn. While, because of the convenience of orderly presentation, we treat them separately, we must always remember that they did not occur in this fashion. They were in process concurrently and interacted upon one another and were also acted upon by what had come down from the nation's past. A thoroughly accurate picture of Japan would be impossible to put down in words or to record on a film. Like the life of other peoples, it was made up of many features, some of them in the background, which moved forward together in inextricable interrelation.

THE ECONOMIC DEVELOPMENT: POPULATION

One of the most obvious and prominently heralded economic features of Japan in the half century after the Chino-

Japanese War of 1894–1895 was the growth in population. At the time when Perry startled Japan out of her isolation, the population of her islands was probably not far from twenty-seven millions. By 1873 it was about thirty-five millions, and by 1893 about forty-one millions. By 1938 it had spurted upward to about seventy-two millions and was being increased at the rate of about a million a year. In other words, it had about doubled in the seventy years before 1935 and had increased by about three-quarters in the forty years before that date.

This increase, while startling, was by no means exceptional. The population of England and Wales had multiplied about two-and-a-quarter times in the sixty years before 1871, and even in the forty years before 1911, when the first effects of industrialization had been felt and the population curve was beginning to level off toward stability, it had risen about sixty per cent. In 1936 Japan had a much smaller population per square mile than did such highly industrialized lands as Belgium, England, and Wales. Nor was Japan's population nearly so dense as that in Java, where a similarly striking growth was being seen, and that in an island where the chief reliance was upon agriculture and where little industrialization had occurred.

However, for Japan the problem presented by the advance in the numbers of her inhabitants was more sobering than that of these other thickly peopled lands. Her population was more than four times as dense as that of China and more than twice as much so as India, both of them countries with overcrowded arable lands. Moreover, because of the mountainous character of her islands only a small proportion of Japan's surface is suited to agriculture. While under the pressure for subsistence more of the soil was being brought under tillage, it was estimated that not more than a fifth of her land could be thus utilized and that in 1931 only about a sixth was thus employed. Much of the four per cent margin was in soil where the returns would only barely compensate for the cost of bringing and keeping it under the plough. Intensive cultivation and extensive application of fertilizers were employed to obtain as much as possible from the acreage. To the traditional night-soil and fish and vegetable sources were added chemical fertilizers. The Government also sought to bring to bear the best of modern scientific agriculture for the benefit of the farmers. However, the system of landholding and of ownership was a handicap. Japanese rice had to compete with that of Korea, where the cost of production was lower. While Japan was manufacturing an increased proportion of her chemical fertilizers, she was largely dependent upon imports for potash and phosphates. In proportion to arable land her population was denser than that of Java, Belgium and the Netherlands, and slightly more so than even England and Wales. It was over twelve times as dense in proportion to arable soil as was that of the United States.

To be sure, there were compensating circumstances. Most of the area which could not be cultivated was suitable for forests and Japan raised much of her needed timber. The rainfall and climate were in general favorable for making the most of the soil. The surrounding seas teemed with fish. The geographic position was such that Japan commanded the water approaches to much of East Asia and was favorably situated for commerce. China was as yet but slightly industrialized and offered a large potential market for an industrialized neighbor which had the advantage over the manufacturing portions of the West in closeness and cheap labor.

Yet even these assets were not without their limitations. Japan was poor in some of the materials essential to industrialization, notably iron and petroleum. The Chinese were not always willing purchasers: their heightened nationalism broke out from time to time in resentful boycotts directed against increasing demands by Japan. In time, and that time might not be long delayed, China herself would be industrialized and would make for herself many of the

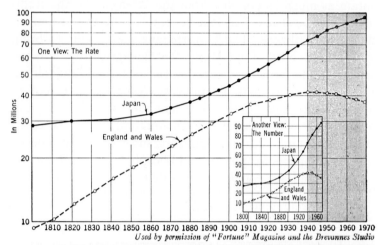

Used by permission of "Fortune" Magazine and the Brevannes Studio

Comparing Japanese and British population growth

products which Japan now sold her and in the 1930's was giving indications of competing in one of Japan's most profitable exports, cotton textiles.

Here in Japan, in other words, were a million more Japanese each year, each of whom wanted more things, and while having some assets, also faced severe handicaps.

One possible door of relief to these pressing millions was all but closed. Emigration on any large scale was out of the question. The Japanese might look with envious eyes upon Australia, New Zealand, and the fertile lands of Canada and the United States, all of them relatively empty as compared with their own crowded acres. While Japan had been wrapped in her self-imposed isolation, however, these lands

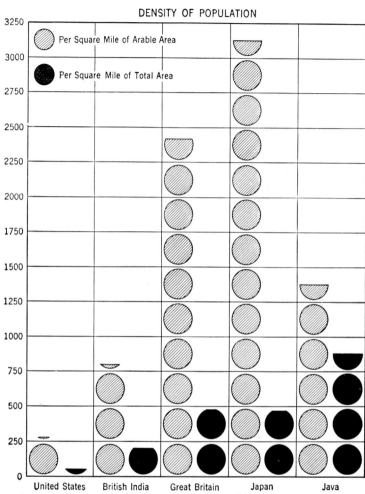

DENSITY OF POPULATION

Per Square Mile of Arable Area

Per Square Mile of Total Area

United States   British India   Great Britain   Japan   Java

Japanese Population Problems

had been taken by the white races. As the first arrivals, these peoples now jealously guarded their shores against a possible influx of Japanese. The Japanese found some outlet in South America, but opportunities there were limited. If they turned to the neighboring continent of Asia, they were there in competition with peoples as able as themselves and with a lower standard of living. Japanese, moreover, seemed averse to leaving home. In 1936 there were only about a million of them outside the empire, and of these more than half were in Manchukuo and the leased territory in that puppet state. Of the remainder, about a quarter of a million were in the United States and Hawaii, and about two hundred thousand in Brazil. The net relief by immigration was much less than a million, for by 1930 more than four hundred thousand Koreans had moved into Japan. Korea was even more congested than Japan, with a lower standard of living, with little outlet through industrialization, and with emigration to Manchukuo and Japan on a larger scale than emigration from Japan Proper.

In time voluntary birth control and smaller families due to that and to delay in the age of marriage would probably bring population to the stationary level which it was approaching in the British Isles, France and the United States. That, however, was in the future and by then the total might reach ninety millions. Whether unexpected developments would hasten or retard the trend no one could confidently predict.

In the meantime, in spite of the yearly augmentation of the population, until she embarked on her large-scale program of war and conquest in the 1930's, Japan was, for a substantial proportion of the population, improving her standard of living. She was doing this in part by the utilization of her food resources. In an amazing fashion she was providing most of her own food. She imported some rice, largely from Korea, and sugar, chiefly from Formosa, but most of her rice, her staple grain, she raised on her own crowded acres. And in the adjacent seas or farther away in the Pacific she caught fish sufficient not only for her own needs but also with a surplus for export. She produced huge quantities of raw silk. This was a supplementary occupation for her overburdened farmers. Three-quarters of the raw silk was usually exported, and of this more than nine-tenths went to the United States. In the years of great prosperity which followed the first World War in the United States, the demand for silk in that country mounted. Japan was using it to help meet her population problem. With the coming of the depression, in 1929 and the 1930's, the American market for silk rapidly deteriorated and with it the price of the Japanese product fell sharply. The effect upon hundreds of thousands in Japan was little short of disastrous. The margin of livelihood of those in the farming districts who had depended upon silk to augment their scanty incomes shrank most painfully. Japan turned to rayon and led the world in its production. This did not, however, immediately benefit those who had been relying upon silk for a livelihood.

The resulting distress, reënforced by other effects of the depression, particularly upon the farming classes, was a contributory cause to the Japanese adventure in Manchuria. From the farms came many of the recruits in Japan's conscript army. They felt keenly the sufferings of their families and communicated their dissatisfaction to their officers. These officers, of junior and middle grades, were mainly responsible for precipitating the enlarged occupation of Manchuria. They apparently expected that they would thus, by enabling Japan to take advantage of the natural resources of the northeastern provinces of China, relieve the economic pressure of the underprivileged in Japan and usher in an era of prosperity. This was not the main source of Japan's expansion, but it was a minor one.

THE CONTINUED INDUSTRIALIZATION OF JAPAN

The chief recourse of Japan in providing a livelihood for her swelling millions and in improving her standard of living was the development of her industries. The farming population remained fairly constant. It was to a phenomenal enlargement of her industries and commerce with the attendant shipping that Japan chiefly looked for economic relief and advance. This meant the growth of her urban centers, already huge, for her industries were concentrated chiefly in Tokyo-Yokohama, Nagoya, Osaka-Kobe, and along the fringes of the Inland Sea. After 1931 the industrial and mining development of Manchuria was accelerated.

Japan's industrialization was partly through the multiplication of small units and partly through the growth of large-scale manufactures. The latter were first textiles and then, latterly, the heavy industries of steel and machinery.

The small-scale industries were to some degree the continuation of traditional handicrafts in silk textiles, lacquer, damascene, potteries, and porcelains, and in part in such newer products as electric lamps, bicycles, and hosiery. Some of the small industries, too, were subordinate to the larger ones.

Large-scale industries were first most extensively employed in cotton textiles. Here was a major export. Indeed, after the slump in the value of raw silk in the 1930's, cotton goods became Japan's main recourse. They went to many different parts of the world, notably to China, India, and the Netherlands Indies. In each of these lands they encountered rivals, and in at least the first two, growing competition from native enterprise.

Later came the heavy industries with the production of

steel, enlarged shipbuilding, and machinery. The production of armaments in the 1930's and 1940's stimulated them to dimensions quite out of proportion to peace-time needs and markets.

Japan's steel industry, centered at Yawata in Kyushu

Black Star

In the large scale enterprises Japan relied in part upon her cheap labor to give her a favorable position in the markets of the world. However, especially in later years, she gave much attention to improved machinery and organization, and to greater efficiency.

For industrial development, raw materials and markets were indispensable. For them Japan had to look largely outside the borders of her home islands. She had a fair supply of coal. Thanks to her many mountain streams, she developed hydroelectric power. She produced much of her copper. Yet she had almost no iron ore and was forced to depend upon imports for iron, steel scrap, pe-

troleum, cotton, some of the basic chemicals for her fertilizers and chemical industries, and much of her copper
and other metals. In time of peace she could be reasonably
sure of a supply of these materials if she were able to pay
for them, for few would refuse a good customer. However,
if she were to pay she must have access to foreign markets.
Here she had difficulty, for many of her products competed
with native industries in the lands where she attempted to

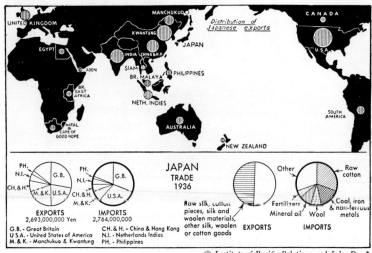

© *Institute of Pacific Relations and John Day* *

The extent and distribution of Japanese trade, 1936

sell, and in a day of rising tariff barriers and of international barter with import and export quotas fixed by inter-
governmental agreements, she had to contest fiercely and
seldom with entire success for outlets for her factories.

The assurance of markets and raw materials was one of
the major motives of her imperial expansion. Japan sought
to make of her empire an economic whole in which she
would be dominant. In general, Japan Proper was to be
the manufacturing center and the other lands in her New

* From " Modern Japan " by W. H. Chamberlin.

Japan's heavy industries and use of electric power contributed much to her military strength.

Order in Greater East Asia were to afford her raw materials and markets. Some industries were developed in China, notably in Manchukuo, but in general the factories were to be in Japan. Could she control the East Indies and the Malay Peninsula she would also have goods of which the rest of the world stood in need — rubber, tin, and quinine. She would then be in a peculiarly favorable position. Economic aspirations were by no means the only ones behind her dream of empire. The ambition of her military leaders, the desire for power, and the thirst for glory were also potent. Yet the economic urge was important.

THE CONCENTRATION OF POWER AND THE DIRECTION OF THE STATE IN INDUSTRY AND COMMERCE

Among the outstanding features of the economic life and organization of Japan were the concentration of much of the capital of the country in the hands of a few families and the growing direction of economic life by the state.

The prominence of great moneyed families was in large part the consequence of government policy in the second half of the nineteenth century. We saw that in the generation following the advent of Perry the state had the leading role in the economic transformation of the country. In exercising this initiative and in meeting its financial problems the government utilized some existing business families. In the process, these family groups augmented their power. Their power increased with the years. They maintained a close connection with the government and each of the two largest associated themselves respectively with the two most influential political parties. The three outstanding groups were important in finance, industry, and commerce, and the fourth was active in banking. They were known collectively as the *Zaibatsu*. Of these the largest were the Mitsui. The Mitsui claimed descent from the Fujiwara, but in Tokugawa times had voluntarily become commoners and entered into trade and money-lending. In the 1860's they discreetly cast in their lot with those who in the name of the Emperor were opposing the Tokugawa. Since the side which they supported triumphed, the government, now in the control of their friends, entrusted them with the management of much of its finances and also sold them, at low prices, properties acquired from the shogun and some

The subway station at Osaka

of the feudal lords. Next in size was Mitsubishi. It also had existed under the Tokugawa. The first development of its fortune was through shipping, in the 1870's and 1880's, but it later branched out into other enterprises. The third,

Sumitomo, had been engaged in Tokugawa times in copper mining and refining and in the rice trade. It continued its metal interests and from them branched out into chemicals,

Aerial cable car at Nikko Mountains

steel and coal mining; from its rice business arose its banking, shipping, and trust activities. Yasuda, the smallest of the big four of the *Zaibatsu*, expanded into banking interests the money lending in which it had been engaged during the shogunate.

MITSUI — JAPAN'S NO. 1 MONOPOLISTS

Here are the interests of the Mitsui, who as bankers, traders, and producers can realistically say: if you don't see what you want, ask for it. The most diversified private capitalist pyramid in the world peaks up at the left in the family holding company Mitsui Gomei Kaisha. In the next rank to the right, from the Mitsui Bank downward, are directly controlled enterprises (by virtue of average stockholdings of 63.4 per cent, loans outstanding, keymen). Branching out from them are their many directly controlled subsidiaries. Farthest right, from the Mitsukoshi Department Stores downward, are companies where Mitsui control is less obvious but nonetheless firmly realistic. The percentages following the names of the largest companies show roughly what part of the *total Japanese business* of that kind is done by the company in question (estimated from paid-up capital of the company as compared with paid-up capital of the whole industry). The chart does not indicate the cumulatively heavy Mitsui investments in government-controlled banks and enterprises, such as the Bank of Japan, the Japan Steel Manufacturing Co., and the South Manchuria Railway.

MITSUI GOMEI KAISHA

Mitsui Bank, Ltd. (5.3%)
Mitsui Life Insurance Co., Ltd. (2%)
Mitsui Trust Co., Ltd. (17.3%) — Sanshin Building Co.
Toshin Warehouse Co., Ltd. (18.9%) —
Taisho Freight & Express

Taisho Marine & Fire (2%)
Nihon Wheat Flour (25%)
Société Anonyme
  Française Bussan
Deutsche Bussan
  Aktiengesellschaft
Mitsui Bussan-
  South Africa (Prop.), Ltd.
Toyo Rayon (15%)
Numazu Woolen Textile
Kyokuto Condensed Milk
Toyo Otis Elevator
Toyo Babcock
Tokyo Accounting & Tabulating Machine Mfg. Co.
Yuasa Storage Battery Co.
Sanki Engineering Co.

Mitsui Bussan Kaisha (42.2%)

Sanken Engineering Co.
Toyo Carrier Engineering Co.
Toyoda Loom Mfg. Co. (3%)
Nihon Mixed Poultry Feed Co.
Tsugami Iron Works
Santai Oil Mills (Dairen)
Toyo Cotton Trading (7%)
Toyo Henshoku Kaisha (knitting)
Showa Seima Kaisha (wool scouring, dyeing, carbonizing)
Anzen Ropeway Co.
Kinoshita Iron Works
Toyo Oil Refining Co.
Toyo Rubber Chemical Industry
Hokukai Lumber Treating Co.
Wakata Briquette Mfg. Co.
Sando Freight & Express
Sanrin Smokeless Coal & Briquette Co.
Chone Ginseng Distributors

Temman Cotton Spinning
Naikai Textile
Hidaka Cotton Spinning
Namboku Cotton
Chuo Textile
Shanghai Cotton Spinning (China)
Toyo Bodah Spinning (India)

Mitsukoshi Department Stores (32%)
Chugai Shogyo Shimpo (newspaper company)
Kanegafuchi Cotton Spinning Co. (14%) { Shanghai Seizo Seishi (silk)
Nambei (S. Am.) Develop.
Showa Sangyo

Dai Nippon Celluloid Co. (4%) { Tokyo Celluloid
Nihon Artificial Leather
Fuji Photographic Films Mfg. Co.

Oji Paper Mfg. Co. (78%)
- Hokkaido Railway (0.3%)
- Nihon Felt
- Nichiro Lumber
- Nakai Co.
- Kyodo Yoshi (paper)
- Dai Nihon Rayon Pulp
- Toyo Paper Mfg. Co.
- Taiwan Paper Mfg. Co.
- Nihon Kimmo
- Kyoei Kigyo
- Roryo Forestry Co.
- Uryu Electric Power
- Karafuto Railway
- Nankwa Railway
- Mansen Development & Electric { Nihon Kako Paper
  Nichiro Lumber
- Oji Securities { Hokkaido Hydroelectric
  Daido Yoshi (paper)
  Karafuto Steamship
- Osaka *Mainichi* (newspaper)

MITSUI GOMEI KAISHA
208

Onoda Cement Mfg. Co. (16.7%) { Oita Cement (5%)
Taihei Cement
Onoda Railway

Mitsui Mining Co., Ltd. (17.3%)
- Kamioka Hydro Electric Co. (1%)
- Miike Nitrogen Industry (1%)
- Toyo High Pressure Industry (1%)
- Claude Process Nitrogen Co.
- Hokkaido Sulphur Mine Co.
- Hokkai Soda Co. (1%)
- Gosei Industry
- Tokyo Metanol

Taiheiyo Colliery Co. (1%)
- Kujiro Rinko Railway Co.
- Keelung Colliery Co. (1%)
- Matsushima Colliery Co.
- Sansei Mining Co.
- Sanko Co.

Shibaura Engineering Works (5.3%)

Hokkaido Colliery & Steamship Co. (10.9%) { Yubari Railway
Kyoritsu Steamship
Muroran Electric Light

Tropical Produce Co. (27.8%)

Nihon Steel Works (3.5%) { Kurobegawa Electric Power (1%)
Mitsui Electro-Chemical Industry (5.3%) { Oyodogawa Hydro Electric
Kyushu Electric Power

Taiwan Development & Tea Producing Co.
Mitsui Ho-on-kai (philanthropic organization)
Izumihashi Hospital and others

Taken from *Fortune* magazine, September, 1936, issue.

The *Zaibatsu* profited by Japan's territorial expansion and made large investments in the overseas acquisitions. Other family groups arose, one or more of them after Japan's adventure in Manchuria in the 1930's, to assist in the development of the new possessions.

The government, supplied with a precedent for active paternalism from the Tokugawa period and the earlier years of the internal transformation of Japan, took an increasingly active part in the economic life of the land, especially in the 1930's and 1940's. The trend in the West after 1914 and particularly after the worldwide depression which had its onset in 1929 was away from the *laissez faire* of the nineteenth century and toward greater government initiative and direction. Japan, sensitive to the climate of opinion in the rest of the world, moved rapidly in that direction. The pace was accelerated by her foreign wars, notably after 1931 and 1937. More and more the government organized and directed industry and trade. As the strain of war upon Japan's economy was intensified, government control was augmented both in large-scale undertakings and in rationing the food, clothing, and other necessities of the millions of private citizens. Japan did not become completely "totalitarian," but the trend was toward that destination.

POLITICAL: THE CHIEF FACTORS

As in many other countries, the political scene was compounded of many rival forces, each struggling for power. As elsewhere, too, the relative strength of the competing elements varied from time to time. Now one would be in power and now another.

The main ingredients in the constantly changing political cauldron were the parties in the lower house of the Diet, the army and the navy with associated patriotic organizations, the civil bureaucracy, the aristocracy, which included the *Genro* or Elder Statesmen, and the *Zaibatsu*. None of these was a complete unit. Each was divided within itself. Yet each was an entity even if at times an inwardly discordant one. Over all, and theoretically above factional strife, was the emperor. Government was in his name and, as in earlier centuries, each aspirant for the control of the nation sought imperial recognition as the means of obtaining and assuring its control. Publicly the emperor could not interfere. Those who became dominant would speak in his name, but it was bad form to induce him to take overt action. Whatever influence he exerted must be in private.

THE ATTEMPT OF THE DEMOCRATIC FORCES THROUGH THE LOWER HOUSE OF THE DIET

Much of the political history of the half century after 1894 had as a prominent feature the attempt of the lower house of the Diet to obtain the kind of control over the government which the House of Commons had acquired in Great Britain. The issue at stake was the triumph of the democratic ideology of the Anglo-Saxon West. Into the details of that struggle we must not take the time to go. They are complex and confusing. The issue was not always clear-cut. Factions and personal ambitions complicated it, as they usually have done in similar contests in other lands.

The chief opponents of responsible parliamentary government were the armed services. They, particularly the army, represented the traditions of the older, pre-Meiji feudal Japan where, from the time of Yoritomo, the military had been dominant. The new order had not unseated them. The leading Western clans, having upset their long-time rivals, the Tokugawa, were dominant in the army and navy — Choshu in the one and Satsuma in the other. They would not lightly relinquish power.

The Chino-Japanese war of 1894–1895 brought a temporary truce. The nation, confronted by a common enemy, for the time being ignored its internal dissensions and gave its attention to the prosecution of the war. The outcome brought added prestige to the army and navy.

However, by partly removing the danger from abroad probably the very ease of the victory contributed to the early renewal of the parliamentary contest. By the close of 1896 Ito, whose ministry had carried through the war, resigned. The constitution had been so drawn that the lower house could not fully enforce its will, yet must be placated if it were not to impede the government. To resolve the impasse, recourse was often had to the proffer of office, or out and out bribery to members of the lower house. The lower house and the struggle between parties thus acquired the reputation of a corruption of which some of its members were not guilty. Cabinets were formed only by a compromise between the various parties in the lower house on the one hand and other elements, chiefly the armed services, on the other.

For a time in the decade which followed the Chino-Japanese war it looked as though Ito had conceded the principle of ministerial responsibility to the Diet. First, on his advice, the Emperor called on Okuma and Itagaki, two of the party leaders, to form a cabinet, and then, when that failed and a cabinet dominated by Sat-Cho (Satsuma and Choshu, and hence the armed forces) also proved short-lived, Ito himself assumed the leadership of the party which had stood for ministerial responsibility. He was again unsuccessful. Other cabinets followed, some of them in which the military were dominant and one in which Okuma, presumably in favor of cabinet responsibility to the Diet, was premier.

Following the First World War there were years when it

The new Diet building in Tokyo

Nakanoshima, the business center of Osaka

seemed that the democratic forces were winning. The outcome of that global struggle had appeared to be a triumph for democracy. Japan, sensitive to world opinion, prepared to conform. In 1918 Hara, a commoner, the first of that class to hold that office, became premier. Although his assassination in 1921 and the consequent downfall of his cabinet was a reverse in the swing toward democracy, in 1925 universal manhood suffrage was instituted and thereby broadened the base of the electorate for the lower house. The enlargement of the franchise was followed by the emergence of a number of parties which advocated more or less extreme social programs and represented radical labor and farming groups with a sprinkling of intellectuals.

However, the parties which continued to poll the overwhelming majority of the votes were those which traced their lineage to predecessors in the early days of the struggle for parliamentary government. These were the Seiyukai, allied with the Mitsui and the land-owning class, and the Minseito, bound up closely with Mitsubishi and industrial interests.

THE GROWING POWER OF THE ARMED SERVICES AND THE
RISING TIDE OF NARROWLY NATIONALISTIC ELEMENTS

From the trend toward democracy there came, late in the 1920's and in the 1930's, a striking reaction. It was intensified as the years passed. It was in large part responsible for committing Japan to a program of imperialistic conquest and, once that program was undertaken, it was in turn strengthened by the necessities of the resulting wars.

The fighting services, and especially the army, had never surrendered their aspirations. Their cause was furthered by national resentment and the dissatisfaction of elements in the population which heightened nationalism. Many had not been able to forget the rebuff at the Paris Peace Con-

Grim-visaged Japanese soldiers on a fatigue assignment

ference when Japan's plea for the endorsement of the principle of racial equality had been denied. The nation, too, was unhappy over the treatment of Japanese in the United States and objected to the abrogation by that country, in 1924, of the "Gentlemen's Agreement" by the prohibition of the admission of "aliens ineligible for citizenship." The refusal of Great Britain and the United States to assent to the principle of the construction by Japan of a navy equal to theirs and their insistence at the Arms Conference in London in 1930 upon the maintenance, with slight modifications in favor of the Japanese, of the ratio agreed upon at the Washington Conference, seemed to many an affront to national dignity. There was also the distress that ensued upon the worldwide economic depression which began in 1929. Japan recovered more quickly from the depression than did most other major nations, for her low-priced goods found a readier market among some of the peoples of the East because of the inability of the latter, aggravated by the decline in their purchasing power, to buy the higher priced manufactures of the West. However, the depression continued to bear heavily upon some groups, particularly upon the farmers who depended for their livelihood upon the production of raw silk. Since silk did not bring its earlier prices in the American market, thousands in Japan suffered and communicated their distress to their sons in the army. A scapegoat was sought and was discovered in the fashion in which Japan had become Westernized and in those classes which favored Western methods.

These various causes of dissatisfaction led many to declare that Japan, in opening her doors to the West and in adopting Western capitalism and parliamentary institutions, had made a tragic mistake. Most of the malcontents were vague as to precisely what measures should be taken, but they were prepared to strike out at politicians and officials who seemed to them to embody treason to Japanese traditions and to support the armed services in their defense of the national honor and prestige and in their attempts to enlarge the empire in such fashion as to relieve economic distress.

The position of the armed forces had been strengthened by

imperial ordinances which gave them a preferential position. That of 1889 on the organization of the cabinet by implication gave the ministers of war and navy direct access to the emperor on "military affairs of secrecy and grave importance" without going through the premier. In 1898 Prince Yamagata, the main creator of the modern army, apparently

Natori, Black Star

The curious compound of Japanese and Western manners and dress

fearing that in the struggle for parliamentary government the civilian officials might obtain control of the armed services, obtained another imperial ordinance limiting the appointment of ministers of war and navy to generals and lieutenant-generals and to admirals and vice-admirals in active service. This meant that the army and navy could, if they so desired, prevent the formation of a cabinet or dictate the terms on which they would accede, for no high ranking officer of either service would or could accept without the consent of his colleagues in the high command. In 1912 the scope of the ordinance was sufficiently relaxed to extend the choice to high-ranking officers on the reserve as well as the active list, but this did not basically alter the situation. Moreover, the power of the armed services was reënforced by a rising tide of nationalism which looked upon the army and navy, and especially the former, as the chief bulwark of the nation and by various patriotic societies. Among the latter were associations of ex-service men, one of them said to have a membership of about three millions. There were, too, many youth organizations of a patriotic nature for the promotion of military training and the military spirit. Some of the societies advocated terrorist measures.

The character of the leadership of the army was being altered by the coming to high position in its ranks of commoners. For the first decades after the abolition of feudalism and the substitution of compulsory military service of all the emperor's male subjects for bearing arms as a privilege of the aristocratic military class, the control of the army and navy remained in the ex-samurai of Choshu and Satsuma. It continued there until after the Russo-Japanese War. As time went on, however, and the officers of this lineage passed off the scene, others came up who were not of the samurai. The training for army posts was narrowly military and imparted little or no understanding of the world at large nor any breadth of knowledge of international relations. As these men came into power the trend in the army became increasingly narrow, supernationalistic, aggressive, and imbued with a kind of mystic patriotism which proved contagious. Some of the outstanding figures lived frugally, appeared to despise wealth, and seemed examples of a stern and single-minded devotion to Japan as embodied in the imperial institution. For a time this trend was not so prominent in the navy, for the education of prospective officers for that branch of the services was somewhat broader than that for army cadets and in the course of their duties naval officers traveled more than did army officers and had more contacts with other peoples. Eventually, however, men of the same narrow stripe as those who were in charge in the army began to come to the fore in the navy.

The army and navy had their hands reënforced by political assassinations. Assassination was by no means a novel feature of Japanese politics. A classic example was that of the Forty-Seven Ronin, famous on the stage and in story, in which the assassins were glorified. There had been numbers of instances in the second half of the nineteenth century in which men, averredly moved by patriotism, had killed or wounded officials. Public opinion usually either regarded them leniently as well-meaning but misguided or fully exonerated and honored them. Now, in the 1930's, came assassinations of high officials, and some of the most notorious of them by army officers.

After 1931 and 1932 when Japan, by her action in Manchuria and her defiance of the League of Nations, was more and more set against the Western world and was exhibiting a war psychology, there spread an epidemic of these murders. In 1930 Hamaguchi, head of the Minseito and premier, was shot by a fanatical youth. Early in 1932 a former minister of finance and the manager of the Mitsui interests were killed. May 15, 1932, a group of young military and naval officers terrorized Tokyo and assassinated the premier. The assassins were given a public trial and were allowed to make long speeches in which they denounced some of the current tendencies in the nation. They were regarded by many as exponents of patriotism and were given light sentences. In August, 1935, a major general, chief of the Military Affairs Bureau, was cut down by one of the "younger officers," a lieutenant colonel, who professed to be acting on a heaven-sent impulse and because of the deplorable state of the country in which farmers were impoverished, politicians corrupt, diplomacy weak, and the emperor dishonored by the naval limitation agreements. This time the assassin was condemned and executed, but not before it became clear that many sympathized with him and that he was expressing the sentiments of many officers in late youth or early middle age of the middle ranks — captains, majors, lieutenant colonels, and colonels. February 26, 1936, an even more spectacular set of murders was perpetrated. The elections for the lower house of the Diet had recently returned majorities for the Minseito with its advocacy of parliamentary government as against fascism and control by the military. This apparently precipitated action which had been contemplated for some time. Several hundreds of soldiers led by lieutenants and captains seized the houses of parliament, the war office, the metropolitan police office, and one of the hotels, murdered high officials, and issued a manifesto in which they declared that the majesty of the empire had been impaired through the growing amassment of wealth by the few at the expense of the many and through the naval agreements, and laid the blame at the doors of the *Genro*, the financial magnates, government officials, and the political parties. The country was shocked by the specter of violent revolution, for a time the army lost in prestige, and a cabinet was formed by the civil bureaucrats.

THE FAILURE OF THE CIVIL BUREAUCRACY AND THE ARISTOC-RACY TO CHECK THE RADICAL MILITARISTS

The radical elements in the army did not immediately gain control of the government. The army itself was not united. Many officers, especially of the older ages and the higher ranks or on the retired lists, were moderates and looked askance at the fire-eaters. Among the officers there were shifting cliques. The civil bureaucracy was powerful. It had its own traditions. Through such branches as the foreign office and the diplomatic service it sought to place a restraining hand upon those of the military who wished to take a short cut to empire no matter what foreign foes they might bring down on their heads. Probably most Japanese wished to extend the empire, or at least greatly to expand Japan's position in East Asia. However, agreement was lacking as to the method and the timetable. The radicals would proceed apace in defiance, if necessary, of the world. The moderates would advance more cautiously and with less obvious display of the mailed fist. At times the foreign office and the diplomats were in ignorance of what the army was planning. They might seem to commit the nation to a course only to have the army or elements in the army frustrate it by independent action.

The ancient aristocracy had influence through its unchallenged social prestige. There were still prominent representatives of that court nobility which had dominated the empire before the rise of the military class and the creation of the *Bakufu*. The last of the Elder Statesmen, Saionji, was a Fujiwara of impeccable social position. He had spent much of his youth in France, and, in general, was a liberal and favored party government. He had been premier in his time and in spite of his advanced age, in the 1920's and 1930's still had great influence. He escaped the purge of February, 1936, but was frail and did not long survive it. In 1937, Konoye, also a Fujiwara, and one time president of the upper house of the Diet, became premier. He did not look kindly upon party government and wished to bring the military into harmonious relations with the cabinet, but he was not an extreme militarist and hoped to preserve the constitution and to remain at peace with the United States.

After 1931 and especially after July, 1937, Japan was increasingly in the grip of war psychology. Japan had embarked upon a foreign adventure that could end only either in domination of Eastern Asia or in probably total defeat. The initial stages of the adventure brought amazing successes. It is not strange, therefore, that Konoye failed and that the military became dominant. As Konoye resigned the premiership a general, Tojo, succeeded him. Under Tojo the nation was more and more regimented. As the pressure of war was prolonged and became more intense, the government, directed by the military, enlarged its direction of every aspect of the nation's life.

THE PERSISTENCE OF THE CONSTITUTION

It must be noted, however, that the constitution was not abrogated and that the Diet continued to meet, though for only short sessions. Even under war conditions the form of parliamentary institutions was maintained. The constitution had not been the creation of a representative elected convention but was the gift of the Meiji Emperor, a ruler whose memory was especially revered. Presumably the constitution could be canceled or amended only by the emperor. The reigning emperor was not disposed to do either, possibly because he was not committed to the extremists among the military and at least partly because to dismiss or alter what had come down from his grandfather would be filial impiety and therefore unthinkable.

THE IMPERIAL INSTITUTION

Through all the changes of the half century before 1914 the imperial institution had continued, as it had from the dim mists of Japan's beginnings. As the years passed it was even more revered. Under the heightened nationalism of the 1930's and 1940's much was made of the emperor and of loyalty to him. The extreme militarists professed to be moved primarily by reverence for him and a desire to bring him glory.

The actual occupants of the throne changed twice within the half century. The year 1912 witnessed the passing of the

Black Star

Hirohito, Revered Son of Heaven, Emperor of Japan, pictured, as customary, on a white horse

Meiji Emperor, Mutsuhito, who had seen the realm through the great changes which had followed his accession and what was known as the Meiji Restoration. He was succeeded by his son, Yoshihito, whose reign period was denominated by Taisho. The Taisho Emperor was progressively unwell and in 1921 his son, the Crown Prince, Hirohito, became regent. Through the death of his father (December, 1926), Hirohito became emperor and the reign period Showa began. The Showa Emperor had traveled abroad before his accession and so knew the outside world by direct contact, the first of all the long succession of emperors to do so. He was known not to favor the extreme measures of the militarists, but could make his influence felt only privately. As the possibility of war increased he became less of a political factor and the militarists used the institution of the emperor to gain support for their program.

SHINTO AND THE DEIFICATION OF NATIONALISM

Patriotism was reinforced and nourished by an intense cult of nationalism represented by Shinto and the teaching of the myths of the origin of Japan and of the imperial house which we noted early in our second chapter.

Shinto, we have seen, was a continuation of religious beliefs and practices which went back to the days, early in the Christian era, before the introduction of Chinese culture and Buddhism. It had persisted, although at times partially assimilated to Buddhism, and had been revived in the later years of the Tokugawa. After 1869 it was greatly strengthened by the new régime. State Shinto was distinguished from sect Shinto. The latter was officially classed with religions, including Buddhism and Christianity, but the former was declared to be purely patriotic and for supervision was placed under a different official department of the government from the others. However, it had gathered about it many of the characteristics of a new religion. It was the cult of the imperial ancestors and of the nation's heroes. To it there were many shrines, including those in schools. Some were especially notable, particularly the one at Ise, associated with the beginnings of the imperial house, the one to the Meiji Emperor, in Tokyo, and the one to national heroes who died in war, also at Tokyo. The reigning emperor as well as his ancestors was considered divine. The imperial pronouncement on education, issued in 1890, based largely upon Confucian ethics and declaring the imperial throne to be of the same age as Heaven and Earth, was read periodically in the schools and with great reverence. Each school had its portrait of the emperor, to be guarded from injury even at the cost of the life of the teacher. Instruction in Shinto, its rites, its deities, and the duties of the subjects to accept them and participate in them as of the essence of patriotism, was made basic in the training of youth. The educated might be aware that the stories of the divine origin of Japan and of the imperial house were myths and not sober history, but they dared not express such opinions, certainly not in periods of war psychology such as afflicted Japan in the 1930's and 1940's.

The general effect of Shinto was to give to the masses and even to the educated an exaggerated sense of the superiority of the Japanese over all other peoples and of the "divine" mission of the country, and to combine this with a fanatical belief in the invincibility of Japan and with devotion to the emperor.

OTHER RELIGIOUS DEVELOPMENTS

Buddhism remained a force, although probably a diminished force, in Japanese life. It was much more vigorous than in either China or Korea. Among its monks were able men, and it displayed some ability in adapting itself to changing conditions and developing new methods and organizations to meet the problems presented by the times.

Sect Shinto, in the form of cults which centered about a particular divinity or which arose from the activities of a founder, flourished. One had its origin in a woman who believed that she received divine messages through automatic writing. Some attained to such wide popularity that

The business center of Osaka shows the influence of the modern architecture of the West.

the government, deeming them dangerous, sought to suppress them.

Christianity recovered from the reverse which it suffered in the 1890's and grew in numbers and influence. Protestantism in its various forms attracted more adherents than either the Roman Catholic or Orthodox Church. The latter, indeed, suffered because of the disasters which overtook the parent body in Russia after 1917. Christianity was predominantly urban and Protestantism drew largely from former samurai and from the professional classes who were especially under the influence of the West. It was mainly of middle class stock. In Kagawa it produced a leader of more than national prominence who was widely acclaimed in Protestant circles in the West. The Japanese desire not to be dominated by foreigners hastened the independence of the Protestant churches of financial aid from the churches of the West and the transfer of administrative posts from Westerners to Japanese. In 1940 and 1941, pressure from the government speeded up the elimination of aliens from administrative posts in the churches and of financial assistance from abroad and brought almost all Protestants into a new, united body called the Church of Christ in Japan. Christians, although less than one per cent of the population, were exercising an influence quite out of proportion to their numbers.

EDUCATIONAL DEVELOPMENTS

Schools based largely upon the learning from the West continued to grow until the strain of the war brought reduction in the student bodies of some of those of middle and higher grade. The elementary course, attendance at which was compulsory, was lengthened from four years to six, and practically all children were enrolled. Universities grew in numbers and size. Technical education was especially popular. Uniform textbooks were adopted and teachers were carefully trained. For years Japan, and especially Tokyo, was the educational center of the Far East. Chinese students once came by the thousands and representatives were to be found from most of the other countries of the Far East. The educational system was not without its problems. Teachers were too frequently underpaid. Funds needed for schools were inadequate because of the urgent demands of the swollen appropriations for the army and navy. The facilities for secondary and higher education were far from sufficient to accommodate all who applied, and there resulted a competition for entrance and for graduation which placed a severe and sometimes unbearable strain upon many of the youths: physical breakdowns and suicides among the student class were alarmingly common. The curricula were in places overloaded and the courses of study too long. Japanese youths, too, were handicapped by having to learn the difficult Chinese characters and a literary language whose style was quite different from the everyday language. Indeed, vocabularies differed so greatly from one field to another that the labor entailed in acquiring more than one tended to keep learning restricted. If he acquired a Western language, as he was compelled to do in the higher schools, the student found the task more difficult than would a European, for the tongue was not like his own. There were more graduates of middle schools and universities than could be absorbed — at least by what in the West would be called the white-collar class. The result was a growing number of unemployed and poverty-stricken intellectuals. Moreover, education was highly regimented. It was made to nourish loyalty to the state. What were termed "dangerous thoughts," notably those of a social, economic, or political nature, were prohibited. Except in the technical

fields of engineering and natural science, independent thinking was discouraged. It was said, moreover, that in spite
of practically universal attendance at primary schools, many,
because of the burden imposed by the use of Chinese characters, lapsed into illiteracy or near-illiteracy in adult life.

In spite of these strictures on the educational systems, Japanese scholars were making notable contributions, including
some in the realms of pure and applied science, disciplines
which had been imported from the West only as recently as
the second half of the nineteenth century.

NEWSPAPERS, THE RADIO, THE CINEMA, AND LITERATURE

The Japanese were a reading people. Great newspapers
were circulated by the hundreds of thousands. There were
two main newspaper groups, the Asahi and the Mainichi
chains. Except in times of national emergency, little censor-
ship was exercised by the police. As war shadows darkened,
especially beginning with 1931, control became more strict,
and the newspapers, usually tending toward the popular and
the sensational, fell solidly into line in the support of the
state and of its foreign policy. The Domei news agency
became in war time or in the period of tension of Japan's
international relations in the 1930's virtually a channel for
such information as the government wished to give out and
a means of official propaganda.

After its introduction the radio spread rapidly and became
almost universal, for although by the end of 1937 only about
a quarter of the families had sets, loudspeakers in central
localities brought broadcasts to nearly everyone. Here, in
the emergency which mounted after 1937, the government
had a means of shaping public opinion.

The cinema became popular. For years many of the films
came from the United States and Europe and, as was true
in other lands where they went, gave to the popular mind

a distorted picture of the West. Films were also made in Japan and strict control was inaugurated over importation of films.

In addition to newspapers, radio, and films that reached almost every Japanese, there were many magazines, numbers of them of a high intellectual standard. For years translations of foreign books multiplied and any book widely talked of in the West, especially of a solid character, was fairly sure to appear in Japanese dress. Japanese were keeping abreast with the thought of the world at large.

CHANGES IN VARIOUS PHASES OF LIFE

In a wide variety of ways many of the superficial aspects of Japanese life continued to be altered in the five decades after 1894.

Until war restrictions on the use of gasoline placed obstacles in the way, the use of the automobile increased, especially in the city. Motor buses became common and continued even after charcoal and other types of fuel had to be substituted for gasoline.

Western sports rose in popularity. Baseball became a national game and drew great crowds. For many years Japanese baseball teams made trips to the United States to play American teams. Japanese tennis champions competed in international matches in the West. Rugby and association football, golf, hockey, skiing, skating, boxing, and field sports had their devotees. Japanese made excellent showings in the Olympic games and held several world swimming records.

Labor unions appeared, although their organization was long officially discouraged, and for a time after 1914 they increased greatly in numbers and membership. For a time Communism of a Russian type had its students and advocates, but in the 1930's the swing in government circles was

against it and it came to be regarded as among the especially "dangerous thoughts."

Women and girls were employed extensively in factories.
Too often they were exploited by pitiless or careless mill-
owners and were compelled to work on excessively long
shifts for hopelessly inadequate wages and to live in surroundings which were a disgrace to the nation. However,

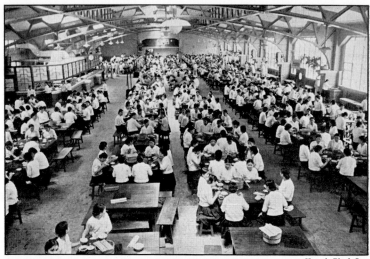

Natori, Black Star

*Japanese workers are regimented in their living arrangements as well as in
their labor.*

legislation was enacted to safeguard labor. For a number
of years Japan was a member of the International Labor
Conference and ratified several of the conventions drafted
under it for the amelioration of industrial workers.

Prostitution had long been present and, as in the West,
was alarmingly aggravated by the shifting conditions of
modern life. The *geisha* (professional entertainers), to be
sure, were beginning to pass, but that was probably chiefly
because none but the well-to-do could afford their services.

In their place was a rapidly growing patronage of cafés and dance halls of the Western type, institutions which were much less expensive than the *geisha*. The relations between the sexes were beginning to change. For a time there was a trend toward the emancipation of women. Women's organizations came into being for obtaining for their sex more of the privileges accorded to men, and there was some demand for the franchise for women. However, with all these changes which, prominent in the rapidly growing cities, met the eye of the Western visitor, the basic fabric of Japanese life was but little modified. The family continued as the fundamental social institution. It still cared for its members and exercised control over them. The traditional position of women in it remained about as it had been for generations, and the individual was kept subordinate to it.

In many ways after 1894 the face of Japanese life was progressively altered. Population mounted, industrialization proceeded apace, cities grew by leaps and bounds, and the outward mechanical trappings of Western civilization were more and more in evidence. Under the pressure of population some of these changes were accelerated.

Beginning early in the 1930's certain aspects of the nation's temper were emphasized. The imperialistic adventure on the adjacent continent, the disapproval of much of the West, especially the United States, the rise of totalitarianism in the West, irritation at the treatment of Japan and the Japanese by Western peoples, and alarm and anger at the growing nationalism and anti-Japanese agitation in China, all contributed to a decline in liberal sentiment in Japan, to the growing control of the more extreme elements in the armed services, to the intensification of hyper-nationalism, and to a rebellion against much that had come from the West.

CHAPTER XIII

Japan Attempts to Dominate Eastern Asia and the Western Pacific (1937–August, 1945)

In the summer of 1937 the intensified clash between Japan and China which had been impending for several years broke out. It was, in reality, a continuation of the struggle which had become acute with the Japanese creation of Manchukuo in 1931–1932. Viewed from the range of a longer perspective, it was a part of the expansion of Japan which in the 1870's had extended the control of the empire over the Kurile Islands, the Ryukyu Islands, and the Bonins. This expansionist trend had led Japan to start the opening of Korea (Chosen). This, of course, prepared the way for the Chino-Japanese War of 1894–1895 with the annexation of Formosa and the Pescadores and the ushering of China out of Korea. The movement continued in the Russo-Japanese War in 1904–1905 with the ensuing footholds in Southern Manchuria, the acquisition of the southern portion of Karafuto, and the incorporation of Korea into the Japanese Empire. The Japanese had sought further opportunity to expand in the World War of 1914–1918 and its aftermath in China, Siberia, and the Pacific and had come out of the struggle with a mandate to islands — the Marianas, Caroline, and Marshall groups — strategically located for the control of the Western Pacific and the defense of the Japanese homeland from the sea.

Even before the coming of Perry, Japan had had her dreamers who advocated the acquisition of empire. Dur-

tension which had been mounting for many years was so great and the resentment of Chinese nationalists so intense that the incident in the North quickly developed into a full scale although undeclared war between the two countries. Compromise was now out of the question. For the Japanese the outcome could be only rule or ruin.

The Marco Polo Bridge, where on July 7, 1937, Japanese forces fired on Chinese troops.

The struggle seemed very unequal. Apparently the military advantages were overwhelmingly with the Japanese. The latter had full command of the sea and could bring in troops and blockade China almost at will. They possessed a large, well-trained, well-equipped, and well-officered army supported by a substantial air force and backed by far the best industrial structure in Eastern Asia. The Chinese, on the other hand, had unlimited man power, but they lacked a fleet, had almost no industry capable of supplying their armies with equipment for a modern war, possessed few aircraft, were without means of replacing those which they had when once they were destroyed, and could bring forward only a small number of officers trained for modern military operations.

It was not surprising, therefore, that the Japanese quickly occupied such of the coast cities as they wished, obtained control of the Yangtze, including Shanghai, Nanking, and Hankow, as far as the gorges which connected Central with West China, and seized most of the railways. Their mechanized equipment and their supremacy in the air and on the water enabled them to take and to hold such centers and facilities as could be dominated by these means.

Only the main outlines of the military phases of the struggle are given here. The fiercest of the fighting was around Shanghai. The Chinese troops made a valiant resistance, but their air force was soon knocked out and large numbers of the best of their troops were killed. By November 9, 1937, the Chinese had begun their withdrawal from Shanghai. Nanking, the capital and architecturally the symbol of the new China, fell on December 12–13, 1937. The wanton brutality of the Japanese toward prisoners of war and the defenseless civilian population in Nanking shocked the civilized world and fanned the resentment and strengthened the will to resist among the Chinese. The Chinese Government moved westward with the remnants of its armies. It established headquarters, temporary as it proved, in Hankow. Hankow was taken by the Japanese on October 25, 1938. The Chinese retreated still farther westward and set up their capital at Chungking, at the western end of the gorges which separated the upper from the lower Yangtze. Through these gorges the Japanese would scarcely venture, for these approaches could be forced by shipping and troops only with very heavy cost, if at all.

The majority of the Japanese expected Chinese resistance now to crumble and hoped to be able to set up a Chinese administration which would coöperate with them. When that did not immediately follow they applied blockade and terrorization. They had already seized most of the Chinese railways, for these were largely in the plains of the lower reaches of the Yangtze and Yellow rivers. On October 21, 1938, four days before their occupation of Hankow, the Japanese moved into Canton. In November, 1938, they took Yochow, above and south of Hankow, and in March, 1939, captured Nanchang, the capital of Kiangsi and a strategic center on the railways between Hangchow on the coast and the through line from Wuchang and Yochow to Canton. In November, 1939, they occupied Pakhoi, a coastal port south and west of Canton, and pushed inland to Nanning, to intercept some of the traffic between French Indo-China and unoccupied China. In June, 1940, they captured Ichang, west of Hankow and near the down river end of the Yangtze gorges. Unopposed in the air, their planes bombed Chinese cities frequently and at will. Their navy blockaded the coast of China.

In the areas subject to their arms, the Japanese set up governments, as they had in Manchuria, headed by those who professed to coöperate with them. For these they were able to attract very few Chinese of character or ability. To head a national administration they obtained Wang Ch'ing-wei. Wang had been a close friend of Sun Yat-sen and may have been regarded by the latter as his spiritual successor. He had been prominent in the Kuomintang, the dominant party in China and the professed embodiment of Sun Yat-sen's program. He had even been in high office in Chung-king, the center of the nationalist government. However, he deserted the latter. His motives were probably mixed and were presumably compounded of personal ambition, of irritation at his colleagues at Chungking, of sincere conviction that China had best make her peace with the conquerors, and of confidence that he could deal successfully with the enemy and establish a régime which would be really independent, although friendly with Japan. With great pomp the Japanese proclaimed, March 30, 1940, the "return" of the national government to Nanking, with Wang Ch'ing-wei as president. They had gone through the farce of having Wang elected by what he claimed to be the orthodox Kuomintang. The Japanese now professed to have what they had desired, a national government of China which would work with them. From the outset, however, it was a broken reed, kept erect only by Japanese support.

CHINA'S CONTINUED RESISTANCE

One of the amazing facts of the thrilling world of the 1930's and 1940's was the fashion in which the Chinese continued their resistance. Space cannot be taken in this survey for even the main outlines of the story. They belong to the history of China rather than of Japan. Here we can simply say that most of the leaders of the nation and many of the rank and file, especially of the well-to-do, the "intelligentsia," and the students, migrated westward to "free" or "unoccupied" China. There they set up their administration, transferred many of their industries and many of their schools and universities, and continued their defense. They not only carried on the war against Japan but also made progress in developing their government, in building roads, in increasing the enrollments in their schools, and in creating new industries. They were not completely united. The communists and the Kuomintang were still opposed to each other and preserved an armed truce as against each other only because of the necessity of expelling the common enemy.

There was much corruption. Mounting inflation menaced the financial structure and bore heavily upon the salaried classes. Most of the railways were in Japanese hands and many of the essentials for modern warfare were lacking. Yet the Chinese were able to hold the Japanese at bay and to take constant toll of their opponents through guerrilla warfare and occasional battles. Where they could use their mechanized equipment the Japanese could maintain their hold. They were not, however, able to push much beyond the railways, the seacoast, and the navigable rivers. Not all of the railway mileage fell into their hands, nor did they quickly occupy all of even the main ports.

THE JAPANESE ATTEMPT SLOWLY TO STRANGLE CHINA

Whether, had they exerted their full force and been willing to pay a heavier price in life, the Japanese would have been able to crush organized Chinese resistance and reduce it to a slowly diminishing guerrilla stage may long be a subject of debate. The measures adopted by the Japanese, whether of necessity or choice, were the slower processes of strangulation by a progressive tightening of their blockade. One after another they plugged most of the possible means of access from "free" China to the outside world, until by mid-1942 the only means by which men and goods could pass from one to the other was by air from India over "the hump" of some of the highest mountains in the world and along the long desert routes from the north-west of China Proper, across the province of Sinkiang, to Russia. In the second half of 1944 a road seemed about to be opened from India, but it was across difficult mountains. The Japanese, too, were then taking large portions of China's remaining railways and were pushing westward into "free" China. By the connivance of officials on both sides, some goods passed

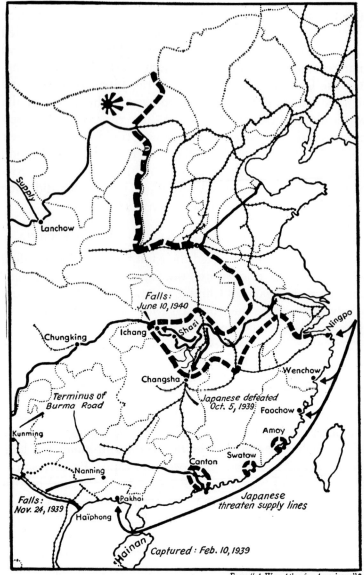

Supply

Lanchow

Falls:
June 10, 1940

Chungking

Ichang   Shasi

Ningpo

Changsha

Wenchow

Terminus of
Burma Road

Japanese defeated
Oct. 5, 1939   Foochow

Kunming

Amoy

Nanning

Swatow

Canton

Japanese
threaten supply lines

Falls:
Nov. 24, 1939

Pakhoi

Haïphong

Hainan   Captured: Feb. 10, 1939

From "A War Atlas for Americans" *

Third year: 1939–40

* Prepared with the assistance of the Office of War Information.   Published by Simon and Schuster.

these two powers. The three agreed to assist one another, Japan recognizing and respecting the leadership of Germany and Italy in establishing a new order in Europe, and Germany and Italy acknowledging the leadership of Japan in bringing into being a "new order in Greater East Asia." They further undertook to assist one another "with all political, economic, and military means if one" of them were "attacked by a power at present not involved in the European War or in the Chinese-Japanese conflict." Since it was specifically stated that the agreement was not to affect the existing political status between "each of the contracting parties and Soviet Russia," the document was clearly directed chiefly against the United States and was a warning to that country to remain neutral. Because the original agreements with Germany and Italy had been an Anti-Comintern pact and an attempt at a safeguard against Russia, Japan valued them mainly as a protection against Russian interference with her program in China. The German "about face" of 1939 in the form of the amazing German-Russian pact brought on a cabinet crisis in Japan. Germany tried to bring Japan and Russia into friendlier relations. The astounding military successes of Germany in Europe gave weight to the arguments of those Japanese who wished to align the fortunes of the Empire more firmly with the Axis. This could be done not only by an alliance with Germany and Italy but also by ceasing the intermittent and undeclared hostilities with Russia on the borders of Manchukuo. In January, 1940, Japan and Russia settled some of their outstanding differences and in April, 1941, under the pressure of German arguments, entered into a neutrality pact. The two agreed to respect each other's territorial integrity and to remain neutral if either were attacked by a third state. The German attack on Russia in the summer of 1941 was still another shock to Japan. However, the Russo-

Japanese neutrality pact was allowed to stand and proved useful to both powers. There was no love in the German-Italian-Japanese alliance. Like most such international arrangements, it was purely a marriage of convenience. Both Germans and Italians despised and disliked the Japanese and the Japanese cherished similar sentiments for their allies. Yet the Axis alliance was something of a shield to Japan in the pursuit of her ambitions.

GROWING TENSION BETWEEN GREAT BRITAIN AND THE UNITED STATES ON THE ONE HAND AND JAPAN ON THE OTHER

By her arrangements with Germany, Italy and Russia, Japan had partly freed her hands for action in the Far East. However, Great Britain and the United States still lay across her path. The British had holdings in concessions, capital, shipping, commerce, and territory of many years standing. Some of these were in China, others were in Borneo and the Malay Peninsula. The recently completed British naval base at Singapore seemed to menace Japan's naval control of the Western Pacific. The United States had never retreated from the Stimson doctrine of faithfulness to the Washington treaties of 1922 with their promise "to respect the sovereignty, the independence, and the territorial and administrative integrity of China" and with their refusal to recognize any situation, treaty, or agreement made contrary to the treaties and agreements of the Pact of Paris, or which would impair the treaty rights of the United States and American citizens. The United States had not officially recognized Manchukuo. She could therefore hardly be expected to view with complacency the alterations which Japan was seeking to work in China and in other parts of Eastern Asia. For reasons of prudence the Japanese Government, while according harsh treatment to the English who were fighting in their home territory with their backs to the wall, sought to conciliate the United States. Many Japanese believed that Britain would need to be eliminated from the Far East but that the United States could be won to Japan's program. The Japanese attempted to browbeat the English in their concession in Tientsin and in the International Settlements in Shanghai and at Kulangsu (off Amoy). They closed the Yangtze against foreign shipping, a measure which bore especially hard on British interests. Some of the British subjects in the zones of Japanese occupation were badly handled. British craft were fired on by the Japanese. The English extended financial aid to China, enlarged the fortifications of Hong Kong, and by their possession of the latter port and of Burma made available channels from "free" China to the outer world. However, their major interests were not in the Far East, but in Europe, India, the Near East, and Africa. Pressed as they were by the Germans, they could spare only small forces for the protection of their holdings in Eastern Asia against a well-armed and determined Japan who was able to concentrate all her energies on that region.

Next to that of China, the main weight of resistance to the fulfillment of the Japanese ambitions was from the United States. From the outset of Japan's expansion in China, even as far back as the World War of 1914–1918, the sympathy of Americans had been with China. To them, Japan was a wanton aggressor at the expense of a weak but potentially strong neighbor. Both American public opinion and the American Government sought to restrain Japan in the earlier world war and its aftermath and in Manchuria in 1931–1932. They were even more strongly against the enlarged invasion of China by Japan which began in 1937. The United States participated in a conference at Brussels in November, 1937, called under the provision of the Nine

Power Treaty (1922) which attempted to compose the differences between China and Japan. Japan spurned the gathering. A movement to boycott the sale of Japanese goods in the United States, while not doing major injury to Japanese imports, was vivid evidence of the American attitude. An organized private effort for "non-participation in Japanese aggression" endeavored to prevent the shipping of gasoline and scrap iron to Japan, for it was well known that these commodities were helping in Japan's Chinese adventure.

The Government of the United States by degrees stiffened its attitude toward Japan. In general it showed great restraint. Early in the Chino-Japanese War, in December, 1937, the *Panay*, an American gunboat in the Yangtze off Nanking, was sunk by Japanese fire. The deed was clearly deliberate, but was probably on the initiative of local officers. The Japanese Government was prompt to apologize and to offer full reparation and many Japanese civilians sought as private citizens to express their regrets and to try to make amends. The American government accepted the apologies. In March, 1938, it withdrew from Tientsin the troops which it had maintained there under the Boxer Protocol of 1901. However, in direct opposition to the Japanese assertion that the progress of events and the inauguration of a "new order" in East Asia had made obsolete earlier treaty arrangements, Washington insisted upon the principle of the open door and declined to recognize Japan's alteration of agreements to which the United States was a party. Washington did not recognize the Wang Ch'ing-wei régime. Relieved of the restrictions of the Washington agreements on the limitation of armaments (at the end of 1936) by the Japanese action in denouncing them, the United States began the expansion of its navy and the fortification of the Aleutians and islands in the Pacific. In July, 1939, acting within its legal rights, the

United States formally denounced its commercial treaty with Japan. On January 26, 1940, after the stipulated notice of six months, the denunciation went into effect and the United States was free to take more vigorous action. A few months earlier, in October, 1939, the American Ambassador to Japan, Joseph Grew, in an address in Tokyo had made it clear that American public opinion was against Japan's actions in China. In 1938 and 1939 the Department of State placed what was in effect a moral embargo upon the shipment to Japan of airplanes and then of plans or plants for the production of high quality aviation gasoline. In July, 1940, an act of Congress made it possible for the President to prohibit the export of munitions and a number of commodities useful for their manufacture and soon after it gave an order requiring licenses for the export of petroleum and its products, tetraethyl lead, and first quality iron and steel scrap. In December, 1940, additional commodities useful in war were placed on the list requiring licenses for export, and on July 25, 1941, under presidential command, both Japanese and Chinese assets in the United States were "frozen," but in such fashion that it was clear that the administration of the order would be so exercised as to strengthen the Chinese economic position. Financial aid was being extended to China by the United States Government through the Reconstruction Finance Corporation and the Export-Import Bank and through Lend-Lease.

JAPAN VENTURES UPON WAR WITH THE UNITED STATES,
THE BRITISH EMPIRE, AND THE NETHERLANDS

It became increasingly clear that Japan was pursuing a path which could only end in war between herself on the one hand and the British Empire, the Netherlands, and the United States on the other. Japan's territorial ambitions as defined by her spokesman extended far beyond China.

Precisely how far they reached was not made clear. Their boundaries were left sufficiently vague to permit elasticity. It was ominous that in 1938 Japan occupied the Paracels Islands and that in 1939 she moved into the Island of Hainan and the Spratley Islands. Since Britain was at death grips with Germany in Europe and seemed to be losing and since the Netherlands and France were under the German heel, the time appeared most opportune to seize their holdings in Eastern Asia and the East Indies. Japan could pose as the liberator of Asiatic peoples from their Western overlords. Whether she would press on to Australia and New Zealand would probably depend upon the degree of her success in the Western Pacific.

As a major obstacle to the realization of Japan's ambitions there loomed the United States. Each power was following a course which, if persisted in, must end in a head-on collision. Japan's program directly opposed the policy to which the United States had been committed for at least half a century, and in principle for a much longer time. That policy had had its strongest expressions in the situation presented by China. On the basis of the Open Door, or opportunity for her citizens equal to that of the most favored nation, the United States had insisted upon the independence and the territorial integrity of China. Encroachments upon China would jeopardize the Open Door. Similarly the Japanese acquisition by conquest of the British, French, or Dutch possessions might curtail the rights of American citizens in trade and investment in these areas. The secretary of state was emphatic that the United States had in no way assented to the French concessions to Japan and opposed the action of Great Britain in closing the Burma Road. When in July, 1941, the German-controlled French Government entered into an agreement with Japan for what was termed coöperation "in military matters for the defense of French Indo-

China," which was a thinly veiled permission to the Japanese to employ that area as a base either for further operations against China or for action against the British and Dutch possessions, the United States voiced its displeasure by giving further aid to China, and through trade measures mentioned above which curtailed greatly American exports to Japan. Moreover, the Japanese government ignored the proposal made by the United States that Indo-China be made a neutralized state.

Some Japanese, including men in high places, hoped to induce the United States not to stand in their way. They held that the United States could be persuaded that it was to her best interests to allow Japan a free hand. Many believed the United States would not fight. It was to keep the United States from belligerency that successive ambassadors to the United States labored and that in November, 1941, Kurusu was sent on a special mission to Washington. Those in control in Japan, however, were resolved to go ahead even at the price of war with the United States.

In November, 1941, it became apparent that only a miracle could prevent war. On November 20, Tokyo presented a group of proposals which suggested that the two countries would undertake to refrain from armed advance in Southeastern Asia and the South Pacific and that Japan would withdraw her troops to northern French Indo-China. But the proposals yielded in no way on China. They stipulated that the two governments coöperate in obtaining the commodities which they needed in the Netherlands Indies, and would pledge the United States "to supply Japan with a required quantity of oil" and to restore relations to the point at which they had been before the freezing of Japan's assets. Japan was clearly determined to continue her reduction of China and to obtain the needed amount of oil. On November 26, Secretary of State Hull handed to Nomura, the

General Tojo, premier of Japan on December 7, 1941, continued in office until the Japanese setbacks in 1944.

Japanese Ambassador, a polite but firm refusal to accept these proposals. He made a counter proposal for the conclusion of a non-aggression agreement among the British Empire, China, Japan, the Netherlands, the Soviet Union, Thailand, and the United States. The United States proposals also provided for an undertaking to respect the territorial integrity of French Indo-China and for the open door for trade in that state; for the withdrawal by Japan from China and Indo-China of all military, naval, air and police forces; for support of the National Government of China; and for the surrender of extra-territoriality, settlements and concessions in China; and rights under the Boxer Protocol. This was to be prefaced by a mutual declaration of policy by Japan and the United States which would embody the principles for which the United States had stood.

On December 7, 1941, the Japanese Ambassador, Nomura, handed to Secretary Hull the reply of his government. It charged the American and British Governments with obstructing Japan's measures to establish "a general peace between Japan and China, with interfering with Japan's constructive endeavors toward the stabilization of East Asia," and with frustrating "Japan's aspiration to the ideal of common prosperity in coöperation with" the Netherlands East Indies and French Indo-China. It accused the American government of desiring to strengthen the "dominant position it has hitherto occupied not only in China but in other parts of East Asia" and declared that the Japanese Government could not "tolerate the perpetuation of such a situation." It ended by saying that the Japanese Government considered it "impossible to reach an agreement through further negotiations."

On that very day and before Nomura and Kurusu had their fateful interview with Hull, the Japanese had launched attacks on the American fleet in Pearl Harbor and the main American airport in Hawaii. That same day they bombed Guam and important centers in the Philippines, destroyed most of the effective American air strength in the latter, occupied the International Settlement in Shanghai, bombed Singapore, and landed forces in northern Malaya. Almost simultaneously Tokyo announced that a state of war existed with the United States and Great Britain. On December 8, 1941, the United States, Great Britain, and the Netherlands Indies declared war on Japan. The war clouds which had been mounting for so many years had suddenly burst in a storm which precipitated the United States, psychologically and militarily only partly prepared, into World War II. Japanese spokesmen declared their objective to be the destruction of the United States and the British Empire.

It was of immense significance for the future that the United States was forced into the Second World War not by way of Europe and the Atlantic, as she had been in the first world conflict, but by way of the Pacific. America's role in the Pacific and the Far East and her importance for Japan were to be augmented to a degree of which few in those momentous December days were aware.

THEY REMEMBER PEARL HARBOR, TOO

In Japan the date that President Roosevelt said would live in infamy is not December 7, 1941, but December 8. On the eighth of each month, throughout the war, the glory of that day was recalled to the Japanese people by government fiat. All newspapers were compelled to display on their front pages, month after month, the full text of the Rescript in which the Emperor declared that he was at war with the United States and the British Empire. Speeches were made in all cities extolling the divine wisdom contained in this document. It is here reprinted in full:

THE IMPERIAL RESCRIPT DECLARING WAR ON U. S. AND BRITAIN

We, by grace of heaven, Emperor of Japan, seated on the Throne of a line unbroken for ages eternal, enjoin upon ye, Our loyal and brave subjects:

We hereby declare war on the United States of America and the British Empire. The men and officers of Our army and navy shall do their utmost in prosecuting the war. Our public servants of various departments shall perform faithfully and diligently their appointed tasks, and all other subjects of Ours shall pursue their respective duties; the entire nation with a united will shall mobilize their total strength so that nothing will miscarry in the attainment of our war aims.

To ensure the stability of East Asia and to contribute to world peace is the farsighted policy which was formulated by Our Great Illustrious Imperial Grandsire and Our Great Imperial Sire succeeding Him, and which We lay constantly to heart.

To cultivate friendship among nations and to enjoy prosperity in common with all nations has always been the guiding principle of Our Empire's foreign policy. It has been truly unavoidable and far from Our Wishes that Our Empire has now been brought to cross swords with America and Britain.

More than four years have passed since China, failing to comprehend the true intentions of Our Empire, and recklessly courting trouble, disturbed the peace of East Asia and compelled Our Empire to take up arms. Although there has been reëstablished the National Government of China, with which Japan has effected neighborly intercourse and coöperation, the régime which has survived at Chungking, relying upon American and British protection, still continues its fratricidal opposition.

Eager for the realization of their inordinate ambition to dominate the Orient, both America and Britain, giving support to the Chungking régime, have aggravated the disturbances in East Asia.

Moreover, these two Powers, inducing other countries to follow suit, increased military preparations on all sides of Our Empire to challenge us. They have obstructed by every means our peaceful commerce, and finally resorted to a direct severance of economic relations, menacing gravely the existence of Our Empire.

Patiently have We waited and long have We endured in the hope that Our Government might retrieve the situation in peace, but Our adversaries, showing not the least spirit of conciliation, have unduly delayed a settlement; and, in the meantime, they have intensified the economic and political pressure to compel thereby Our Empire to submission.

This trend of affairs would, if left unchecked, not only nullify Our Empire's efforts of many years for the sake of the stabilization of East Asia, but also endanger the very existence of Our nation. The situation being such as it is, Our Empire for its existence and self-defense has no other recourse but to appeal to arms and to crush every obstacle in its path.

The hallowed spirits of Our Imperial Ancestors guarding Us from above, We rely upon the loyalty and courage of Our subjects in Our confident expectation that the task bequeathed by Our Forefathers will be carried forward, and that the source of evil will be speedily eradicated and an enduring peace immutably established in East Asia, preserving thereby the glory of Our Empire.

JAPAN'S RAPID ADVANCE

The initial advantage clearly lay with Japan. She was thoroughly prepared. The British Empire, its forces strained to hold the Germans and Italians at bay, could bring but little of its great might against the Japanese: it would have to be content with standing on the defense and in very vulnerable positions. The Dutch in the Netherlands East Indies offered valiant opposition but from the outset were foredoomed. The United States had been dealt crippling blows in its sea and air forces and for the present would need to give its major attention to the Atlantic and Europe, for Pearl Harbor had been quickly followed by war with Germany and Italy and the armies of these enemies appeared triumphant. It would take time to arm and to make effective her huge strength. Japan had the advantage, too, of geographic position. Vast distances protected her against the full might of the United States and the British homeland and dominions. She had carefully trained her army for the kind of jungle fighting and amphibious warfare called for by her southern ambitions. By prompt action she could easily seize the British, Dutch, and American possessions in the Western Pacific and the East of Asia.

The progress of the Japanese in the closing days of the year 1941 and the early part of 1942 was phenomenal and erased for the time being the colonial holdings of the Occident in Southeastern Asia, except the remnants of French control in Indo-China and the small Portuguese possessions at Macao and in Timor. Even Timor was occupied early, to forestall similar action by the Dutch. On Christmas Day, 1941, less than a month after Pearl Harbor and not quite a hundred years after the cession of the island to Great Britain by China, Hong Kong fell. On the same day the Japanese seized the capital of Sarawak, a British protectorate in Borneo. The Japanese moved rapidly down the Malay Peninsula, in spite of desperate British resistance, and on February 17th received the unconditional surrender of Singapore with its supposedly impregnable naval base. They thus extinguished a British colony which reached back to the Napoleonic wars. Before the end of January Japanese had obtained a foothold in the northern end of the Solomon Islands and were threatening the communications between the United States and Australia. Guam had been seized a few days after Pearl Harbor and within a few weeks Wake Island had been reduced after the heroic resistance of the small American force. The Netherlands East Indies were attacked at a variety of points. British, Australian, and American ships, Australian troops, and American aircraft were rushed to reinforce the defense, but, after fierce but

The Japanese were proud of their navy, which grew rapidly after the coming of Perry and proved itself in the war with Russia.

260

brief fighting, these, with the Dutch forces, were annihilated or scattered. By the middle of March Batavia had fallen and the conquest of the East Indies had been virtually accomplished. Several ports in the northern part of Australia were being bombed by the Japanese and the invasion of that dominion appeared to be impending. Before the middle of March, moreover, the Japanese had driven into Burma, Rangoon had been taken, the British forces were retreating into northern Burma, and the pitiful flight of Indian civilians from Burma had begun across the mountainous jungle trails to Assam. Japanese had early attacked the Philippines at a number of points. The chief defense was on the Bataan Peninsula, near Manila. Here, cut off from any possibility of effective reënforcement, a vastly outnumbered army of Filipinos and Americans fought one of those losing battles which go down into history with more glory for the vanquished than victors, and held out until April 9th. Before the final surrender, the commander, General MacArthur, in obedience to orders had escaped to renew the combat from Australia and the South. The Island of Corregidor, the last stronghold near Manila, surrendered on May 6th after bitter fighting. Elsewhere in the Philippines scattered resistance was kept up for months, but the islands were now clearly in the hands of Japan. In April the Japanese navy was operating in the Bay of Bengal and Japanese planes were bombing Ceylon. Before the end of May the Japanese were masters of Burma, and had effectually closed the Burma Road, cutting off that passage between the Chinese and the outer world.

Within less than six months after their startling attack on Pearl Harbor the Japanese had wiped out British and Dutch power from the Far East, the East Indies, and Southeastern Asia to the borders of India and had made themselves masters of the American-protected Philippines and of American outposts in the Western Pacific. Before the end of June they had established footholds in the Aleutians and were attacking Dutch Harbor. The dizzy course of victories over the greatest naval powers of the world might well seem to assure the Japanese of the domination of which they dreamed.

JAPANESE ATTEMPTS TO CONSOLIDATE AND TAKE ADVANTAGE OF THE CONQUESTS

Japan strove to take advantage for her own benefit of the economic resources of the lands which had so rapidly come into her possession and to consolidate her power in such fashion that she could not be easily dislodged. She talked first of a "new order in East Asia" and then, as her program expanded, of a "Greater East Asia co-prosperity sphere." Her ambition was to weld her conquests into an economic whole in which, in theory, all the peoples would prosper, and in which, in general, Japan and possibly to a smaller extent Manchukuo and parts of China would be the industrial centers and the other lands provide the raw materials. To this end large corporations were developed, somewhat akin to what had been used in Korea and Manchuria. Among these were the North China Development Company, the Central China Promotion Company, and the Greater East Asia Development Corporation. In practice, the Japanese exploited the occupied regions for their own benefit rather than that of the conquered peoples. Their armed forces were followed by private adventurers or representatives of companies seeking goods and profits. Paper currencies were circulated which were supported only by coercion and which rapidly depreciated. These were used in payment for Japanese "purchases." In the occupied portions of China the traffic in opium and opium derivatives flourished through at least the connivance of the Japanese authorities and to the profit of Korean pedlars, Japanese dealers, and, supposedly, of Japanese army officers. There were dissensions between the Japanese army and the Japanese navy, each attempting to seize the choice plums. Along the China coast and across the shifting and blurred borders between "free" and "occupied" China smuggling proceeded to the advantage of Japanese officers and officials. The Japanese made much of their purpose to liberate the peoples of East Asia from the white man's yoke. They professed to abolish the special foreign concessions in China's ports, to give independence to the Philippines and to Burma, and to further the liberation of India. In actual practice they continued to operate through puppets and had open contempt for at least some of the peoples in the lands under their control. Thailand, although theoretically independent and gaining territorially by Japanese friendship, felt the heavy hand of her all-too-powerful ally. Reports came out from various lands of forced labor and of harshness unparalleled in the recent history of the Western administrations Japan was not winning the affections of her new subjects.

THE COMPULSORY EBB OF THE JAPANESE TIDE BEGINS

The phenomenal Japanese conquests had not been made without cost to themselves. The adventure in China, particularly since 1937, had taken heavy toll in life and tronoure. It had not been as exhausting as some optimists among the Chinese and their friends had predicted. Yet it was a drain on Japan's resources in men and money which was as yet only imperfectly balanced by economic returns. The early victories over the British, Americans, Dutch, Australians, and Filipinos had been achieved at a not inconsiderable price, particularly in ships.

Japan's opponents, recovering from the shock of initial defeat, began to gather their forces to recover the lost ground and to subdue their enemy in her home territory.

The Japanese army, shown in review, was modeled on that of Germany.

They were taking the initial steps on the road to Tokyo. That road might be long, but they professed determination to fight their way along it to its destination.

China's resistance continued. Here and there the Japanese drove their lines farther into Chinese territory, but usually only to be forced back by the resurgent Chinese. The difficult air route over "the hump" from West China to India was utilized by planes of American origin, and by 1944 more freight was coming over it monthly than had ever been brought over the Burma Road. An increasing American air force, with the necessary equipment, was being flown to China, and air fields for it were being constructed at strategic points. From these fields American and Chinese planes — the latter also from the United States — were bombing Japanese centers in China, Indo-China, and Formosa and Japan itself and were effectively disputing the Japanese mastery of the China air. Yet, deprived of her foreign commerce and of some of her richest territories, and burdened with war, China was suffering from run-away inflation, and her auto transport, a main reliance, was rapidly deteriorating.

The British assembled forces in India, and by 1944 they had made sorties into Burma by air and land and their submarines had begun to sink Japanese shipping. Their navy, too, was operating in the Indian Ocean and against Sumatra.

Australian forces, partly in conjunction with those of the United States, drove back the Japanese in New Guinea, thus ending the threat of immediate invasion of their homeland and preparing the way for further advances against the enemy.

The British, however, had their hands full nearer home, and even the Australians, in spite of the Japanese invasion of their colonial possessions and the menace to their own continent, had already mortgaged a large part of their somewhat limited resources to the defense of the British Empire in the Near East and the Mediterranean. Britain promised that, once the European phase of the struggle was successfully completed, she would give her major attention to the defeat of Japan, but for the time being the Pacific must be for her incidental and neither Australia nor New Zealand could concentrate on it with undivided attention.

The United States, in spite of the fact that her strategy in World War II called for giving priority in her resources to the defeat of Italy and Germany, was able to bring a part of her rapidly growing armed might to bear on the Japanese. Her navy through its surface ships took toll from its Japanese rival. In the Battle of the Coral Sea, between the Solomon Islands and New Guinea (May, 1942), and in the Battle of Midway (June, 1942) the American navy inflicted striking defeats on the Japanese and prevented the extension of Japanese power southeastward and eastward. American submarines ranged far, even into the home waters of Japan, and sank hundreds of Japanese vessels, thus crippling Japan's access to her farflung conquests and overseas forces. In the spring of 1942, an American air force raided Tokyo. In the summer of 1942, by bitter amphibious warfare, Americans won a foothold on Guadalcanal, in the Solomons. In the succeeding months the American advance from the South continued, usually preceded by air attacks which destroyed Japanese ships and planes, sometimes accompanied by minor naval engagements, and made permanently effective by the occupation of island posts. By the spring of 1944 the Americans had advanced into the New Britain Archipelago and the Gilbert and Marshall Islands, and had repeatedly bombed Japanese installations to the west of these points, including the important naval base of Truk, in the Carolines. In 1943 the Japanese were compelled to retire from the Aleutians and by the spring

fore in historic times had an invader set foot on the soil of the islands. The myth of invincibility and inviolability on which the Japanese had been nurtured had been rudely shattered.

Yet the Japanese submitted. No uprisings threatened the rule of SCAP. That was partly because the Emperor loyally cooperated and commanded his subjects to submit. It was also because the nation was exhausted, both emotionally and physically. During the first few months the feelings of a large proportion of the population were compounded of relief and stunned apathy. Some even welcomed the occupation. The extreme militarists were now unpopular. Thousands held them responsible for having brought the nation to its tragic plight. Even control by the victor was thought to be better than a continuation of the strain of the long and losing war. After the decade and a half during which the nation had been whipped up and regimented by its military leaders to implement the dream of "Greater East Asia," it was near to economic and mental collapse. For the moment millions were dulled as by a kind of mass shell shock. Enemy bombings had wrecked most of the industrial plant of the nation, a plant already overstrained by the war effort. To achieve the barest physical subsistence was a struggle. The aid given by the conquerors was gladly or passively accepted.

The changes wrought by SCAP were drastic. Never before had foreigners undertaken the remaking of so numerous a civilized people on so thoroughgoing a scale. To effect the changes a large staff was assembled and organized. Its personnel was predominantly American, but a few from others of the Allied Powers were included. The Far Eastern Commission endeavored to exercise control, but it sat in distant Washington; and the masterful MacArthur, on the ground, usually found ways of doing what he believed wise.

In theory, and to a large extent in practice, SCAP acted through the Japanese Government. MacArthur's principle was that he was there to help the Japanese to work out the needed reforms, but in none too subtle ways he made it clear what he believed was required. For the time being the Japanese acquiesced. In their exhaustion they welcomed a strong hand, especially since it so clearly had their welfare at heart. Something of a precedent existed in the ablest of the shoguns: they had acted through the Emperor but he had been a puppet in their hands.

The problems which confronted SCAP and the Japanese were formidable. The Japanese armies had to be brought home and demobilized. The several militaristic and chauvinistic groups which had urged Japan on in her mad imperialistic adventure must be dissolved. It was important to devise a way of bringing back from Russia the thousands of Japanese who had been taken prisoners in the closing days of the war. The economic situation, already grave before the war, was very much more acute. Bombings of the cities and the accompanying fires had destroyed thousands of homes and rendered hundreds of thousands all but shelterless. Supplies of food, greatly reduced during the war, were even less adequate to feed a population which continued to mount. Indeed, the health measures introduced by SCAP were followed by a steep increase. The predicted curve (p. 196) was being approximated. The amount of grain raised in the country was quite insufficient, and the calorie content of the already Spartan rations had to be reduced. Defeat had deprived Japan of overseas possessions on which she had depended for food, raw materials, markets, and some of her manufactured goods: she had lost the Kuriles, southern Sakhalin, the Ryukyus, Korea, Formosa, and her holdings in South Manchuria and the mid-Pacific. Her merchant marine, on which she had leaned heavily, had been destroyed. The machines on which she had depended for goods to exchange for food and raw materials were worn out, obsolete, or blown to bits. Inflation had the currency in its clutches. Japan's chief prewar market, China, had suffered from her aggression and was virtually closed, first by the Nationalists and then by the Communists. Smarting under the memory of the recent occupation, the peoples of Southeast Asia were reluctant to trade with Japan, and for the time being were themselves gripped by postwar poverty. But the country must be so reconstructed that it would be safely set on the road to economic stability and democratization.

In the face of these obstacles the achievements of the next few years were notable. They were due in part to SCAP and in part to the Japanese themselves. Japan's armed forces were demobilized and brought home. The ultrapatriotic societies were dissolved or driven underground. After delays due to the Russians, a large proportion of the prisoners was repatriated. In the meantime many of them had been indoctrinated with Communism, and presented a fresh problem. Government, business, and education were purged of those who were regarded as leaders in the country's war-making program. Those deemed war criminals were brought before courts. Some trials were by military tribunals in the lands where the offenses had been committed. The one which attracted most attention was in Tokyo, before what was called the Military Tribunal of the Far East. It continued for several months, and in November, 1948, found all the accused guilty of planning a war of aggression. Seven were condemned to death and the others to imprisonment. To meet the immediate economic situation, food was imported from the United States and efforts were made to curb the rapidly mounting inflation.

A new constitution was promulgated in November, 1946, and became effective the following May. In theory it was framed under directives from the Far Eastern Commission in Washington and was adopted after free discussion in the Japanese Diet. Actually, the document which was finally accepted was written by SCAP and bore the strong impress of MacArthur's hand. Preliminary attempts by the Japanese had produced drafts which MacArthur deemed too conservative. He stepped in, and in two days of conferences between SCAP officials and Cabinet representatives a draft was produced which passed the Diet with some amendments.

As promulgated, the new constitution, in contrast with the one of 1889 which was expressly the gift of the Emperor, declared that it was the act of the Japanese people through their elected representatives in the Diet. It insisted that sovereign power resided in the people and that the Emperor was the "symbol of the state" and derived his position from the will of the people. The advice and approval of the Cabinet were required for all acts of the Emperor. The Cabinet was to be dependent on the Diet. A long section, which was in effect a bill of rights, declared the people to have fundamental rights. Among them were equality under the law, the power to choose and dismiss public officials, universal adult suffrage, the secrecy of the ballot, freedom of peaceful petition, of thought, conscience, religion, assembly, and speech; the right of equal education, and the right to maintain "the minimum standards of wholesome and cultured living." The right of workers to organize and to bargain and act collectively was guaranteed. The right to own or hold property was declared to be inviolable. There were to be no peers or peerages. There was to be a Diet made up of a House of Representatives and a House of Councilors. The members of both were to be elected. By a two-thirds vote the lower house might pass a measure over the veto of the upper house. The Prime Minister was to be chosen from the members of the Diet, and he and all the Cabinet ministers were to be civilians. The Cabinet was responsible collectively to the Diet and was invested with all executive authority. The judiciary was made independent of the executive. A provision of the constitution which was later to embarrass both the Government and the United States declared that "the Japanese people forever renounce war as a sovereign right of the nation and the threat or use of force as means of settling international disputes. . . . Land, sea, and air forces, as well as other war potential, will never be maintained. The right of belligerency of the state will not be recognized."

With the permission of SCAP, political parties were revived. They did not follow exactly the prewar patterns, and a Communist Party appeared. In the main the electorate was conservative, and elements from the Seiyukai and Minseito appeared under other names and combinations.

Under the constitution the support of the Shinto shrines by the Government was impossible. Thus a notable bulwark of intense nationalism was crippled. However, the shrines of what had been state Shinto were maintained by private contributions, and continued to be frequented.

The institution of the Emperor was retained. Among some of the conquerors there was a move to abolish it. However, the counsels of those who favored its continuation prevailed. But even before the adoption of the new constitution Hirohito by rescript denounced as fictitious the ideas that the Emperor was manifest god and that "the Japanese people are a race superior to other races and therefore destined to rule the world." Nevertheless, reverence for the Emperor persisted.

On the economic front SCAP adopted drastic measures. The *Zaibatsu* were ordered dissolved. Thus the domination of Japan's finance, commerce, and industry by monopoly power was to be ended. However, the purpose was not fully carried out. More lasting was the redistribution of agricultural lands. Landlordism had long been a palpable evil. Nearly three-fourths of the cultivators of the soil were renters, often from absentee owners, and their rent was equal to half or more of the annual crop. In 1946 legislation was passed which required absentee owners to sell their holdings to the Government. Tenant cultivators could buy the land they tilled in thirty annual installments at low interest. Rentals were not to exceed a fourth of the crop. Few holdings were to exceed 7.5 acres. Non-cultivators who lived on their land could retain 2.5 acres. Under this program, by 1950 three million cultivators obtained possession of about five million acres. Here was a little heralded agrarian reform as notable as that carried out by the Communists in China and without the forcible liquidation of hundreds of thousands of individual landlords entailed in that much publicized program.

Under SCAP the police system was decentralized. Previously it had been under the direct control of the Home Minister and had been a main support of a militaristic, autocratic régime. Now it was divided between municipal police, locally controlled, and rural police under national administration.

The educational structure was remade. It had been a major support of chauvinistic nationalism. Teachers who were known as ultra-nationalists were dismissed, and textbooks in geography and history either were revised or were replaced by new ones. Individual initiative, equal educational opportunity, and academic freedom were stressed. Schools were to be under local boards elected by the communities. They were crowded. Under the demand for secondary and higher education and an inflation which bore hard on teachers' salaries, enrollments mounted to match costs with tuitions and in many institutions academic standards suffered.

A long-unsolved problem was reparations. Peoples who had been subjected to the Japanese invasion demanded them. Not until after the end of the occupation were agreements made which finally settled the issue. However, under SCAP some payments were made by the transfer of surplus facilities of war industries.

Economic recovery was gradually but only partially achieved. Imports exceeded exports. The United States Government felt that it must aid the rehabilitation of the country. From September, 1945, to July, 1950, it gave aid in food, fertilizers, chemicals, and other goods to the sum of nearly $1,375,000,000. When, in the summer of 1950, war broke out in Korea, and the forces of the United Nations moved in to repel the attack, Japan became geographically the most convenient place to procure supplies. The purchases gave a welcome but only temporary stimulus to Japanese industry. The hard-working Japanese rebuilt their cities and revived their manufacturing plants. Slowly but fairly steadily the margin between imports and exports was reduced. Some foreign markets were regained. For a time the United States was the best purchaser, not of raw silk, as had once been the case, but of manufactured goods. As early as December, 1948, at the behest of SCAP, the Japanese Government took steps to balance its budget, to reform its tax structure, to increase production, and to stabilize wages and prices.

CHAPTER XV

Japan Regains Her Independence but Is Still Bound Closely to the United States

As early as 1947 negotiations were begun for a general peace treaty. However, the U.S.S.R. and Communist China made demands to which the United States was unwilling to accede. Members of the British Commonwealth pressed for a treaty, and in 1950 negotiations were reopened, with John Foster Dulles, later to be Secretary of State, as the chief American agent. Eventually a document was drafted. Under it, Japan recognized the independence of Korea, renounced all claims to Formosa, the Pescadores, the Kuriles, southern Sakhalin, and the Pacific islands which had been under her mandate. She agreed to placing the Ryukyu, Bonin, and Volcano islands under a United Nations trusteeship. The treaty was signed by forty-eight nations and Japan in San Francisco on September 8, 1951. Burma, India, and Yugoslavia refused to attend, and the U.S.S.R., Czechoslovakia, and Poland were represented but did not sign. The U.S.S.R. had insisted, in vain, that the (Communist) People's Republic of China be invited. The U.S.S.R. abstained partly for that reason and partly because it said that the treaty bound Japan too closely to the United States. By the middle of 1952 a sufficient number of governments had ratified the treaty to permit it to come into force. Thereupon the occupation came to an end, and Japan regained her full independence. In April, 1952, Japan and Nationalist China, now ensconced on Formosa, signed a treaty of peace. Burma and Indonesia had declined to sign the San Francisco document because in their judgment it did not require Japan to make sufficient reparation for the damage done them during the war. In 1954 the Philippines ratified the document, but not until after an agreement had been reached with Japan on reparations. In the general treaty of peace Japan agreed to accept the obligations of the Charter of the United Nations for the settlement of international disputes and to refrain from the threat or use of force, but the Allied Powers recognized her right of self-defense.

In 1951 the United States and Japan entered into a security pact through which the United States was to maintain bases to protect that country, still unarmed, against attack from abroad. Under pressure from the United States and with American aid Japan undertook the beginnings of rearmament. In March, 1954, the two signed a Mutual Defense Assistance Agreement. By it, Japan was to contribute "to the development and maintenance of its own defensive strength and the defensive strength of the free world," the United States was to give military aid in goods, equipment, and services, and both were to keep a close curb on their trade with Communist China. Rearmament, so contrary to the constitution recently adopted on the insistence of the United States, aroused much controversy in Japan. Many opposed it on the ground that it could well be the prelude to renewed militarism and the return to power of the military. The Communists joined in the criticism.

Release from the occupation did not mean reversion to prewar conditions. Not all of the changes adopted under SCAP were retained, but some persisted. It became clear that the occupation had speeded developments which were already under way before the militaristic and imperialistic spasm of the 1930's and the fore part of the 1940's. Women would not surrender the equality granted by the new constitution. The fruits of land reform were largely but not entirely preserved. Labor organizations continued. Yet modifications in the SCAP innovations were made. In July, 1952, to enable the government to curb disorder, an Antisubversive Activity Law was enacted. For the same purpose the decentralization of the police force was reversed and the Government obtained greater control over that arm of administration. Restrictions were placed on teachers and on the freedom of education. Large financial combinations appeared which in some degree were a revival of the *Zaibatsu* tradition. The Prime Minister made a formal visit and announcements to the imperial shrines at Ise. Yet the clock was by no means completely turned back.

Internationally Japan was not relieved of perplexities. Though many Japanese pressed for commercial relations with Communist China, by mid-1956 no treaty had been negotiated with that régime. Nor was there as yet a peace treaty with Russia. As a condition for such a settlement, Japan made demands for the return of territory which the U.S.S.R. would not concede. Moscow blocked Japan's admission to membership in the United Nations. There was serious friction over fishing rights with the Republic of Korea. This entailed the control of the seas between the two countries. Many Japanese were apprehensive over the cold war between the Communist bloc and the United States. They feared that in the event of war their Mutual Defense Assistance Agreement with the United States would place them on the front line and that in the atomic age their vulnerability would entail even greater destruction than in World War II. They longed to hold a neutral position. Much criticism of the United States was voiced. The presence of American armed forces was a chronic irritant. The testing of atomic weapons by the United States in the Pacific, and the resultant contamination of fish which were a major item in the Japanese diet, for a time aroused a near approach to national hysteria. Organizations of veterans with a possible renewal of militarism raised their heads. Demands began to be heard for the return of the Ryukyus and the Bonins.

On the whole, in domestic politics Japan remained conservative. The Communists infiltrated several organizations, among them student and labor groups, and were vocal in objurgation of the American connection, but they won few seats in the Diet. In the elections the conservative parties had large majorities. The traditional fear of Russia continued. The parties were grouped as much around individuals as around principles and were troubled by internal factions, but parliamentary government was maintained.

There was much religious ferment. Buddhism was further weakened by the loss of endowments of temples and monasteries in the redistribution of the land. For the first few months after August, 1945, marked interest was shown in Christianity: many asked whether here was the source of the strength of the victors and of the potency of democracy. Hundreds of Christian missionaries entered the country. Yet the growth of church membership was not spectacular, and Christians numbered only about one in two hundred of the population. The revival of religion was chiefly through the growth of Shinto and syncretistic cults.

Some progress was made toward solving economic problems. Population still mounted. In 1953 it was estimated at 86,300,000. Yet various methods of birth control were being widely practised. In the mid-1950's imports still exceeded exports, but production was higher than before World War II and foreign sales were growing. For example, shipbuilding was reviving and ships were being built for the foreign market. For some groups, including the coal miners, conditions were still grim, but decided improvement in the over-all picture had been registered.

Japan was changing, but the disruption from the past was not sharp. Much of the old remained.

APPENDICES

APPENDIX I

SOME SIGNIFICANT EVENTS IN JAPANESE HISTORY *

Chronology

Political Evolution	Japanese periods	Japanese dates	Western dates	Chronology
PATRIARCHAL PERIOD of self-sustaining clans.	LEGENDARY PERIOD		660 B.C.	Founding of the Japanese Empire by Emperor Jimmu.
		Chuai 9	200 A.D.	Korean expedition of Empress Jingo.
		O-jin 15	284	Japanese court sends to Paikché (Korea) for scribe Wani. (Official adoption of Chinese script follows.)
	YAMATO	Kim-mei 13	552	Paikché sends image of Buddha, volumes of the sutras, and, in 554, men learned in the classics, medicine, divination, etc.
		Suiko 12	604	Shotoku Taishi, regent for Empress Suiko, issues a code, first formulation of law in Japan.
BUREAUCRATIC SYSTEM imported from China (646), changing shortly to ARISTOCRATIC SYSTEM with one dominant clan family assuming regency.		Taikwa 2	646	Nakatomi no Kamatari (founder of the Fujiwara family) formulates the Taikwa reform edict, in essence the application to Japan of the centralized bureaucratic system of the Chinese Empire.
	NARA	Wado 3	710	Nara, first permanent capital, laid out on model of the Chinese capital.
		Tempei 13	741	Buddhism becomes in effect the state religion.
	HEIAN	Enryaku 13	794	After ten years of building a new capital at Nagaoka, Emperor Kwammu switches to Kyoto, five miles distant, and rebuilds his capital there.
		Enryaku 21	802	Successful campaign against the Ainu, indigenous barbarians in the north of Japan.
		Bunji 1	1185	Taira clan defeated at Dan-no-ura; Minamoto no Yoritomo supreme in Japan. Struggle between Taira and Minamoto clans. Epic period in Japanese history. Formation of samurai caste.

* Taken from *Fortune* magazine, September, 1936, issue.

Period	Era name	Year	Event
KAMAKURA	Kenkyu 3	1192	Yoritomo made Sei-i-Tai-Shogun (Barbarian-Subduing-Generalissimo); sets up Bakufu (military headquarters) at Kamakura, in eastern Japan.
	Shoji 1	1199	Hojo Regency begins on death of Yoritomo.
	Shokyu 1	1219	Fujiwara puppet Shogun set up in Kamakura.
	Bunei 11	1274	First invasion of Japan by Kublai Khan.
	Ko-an 4	1281	Second invasion.
	Genko 3	1333	Emperor Go-Daigo destroys Kamakura; Hojo Regency ends with suicide of last regent.
NAMBOKO-CHO	Engen 1	1336	Rival courts: Go-Daigo establishes "Southern" Court; Ashikaga Takauji sets up Emperor Komyo in Kyoto.
	Genchu 9	1392	Half-century struggle over succession, fundamentally a redistribution of feudal power, ends with Ashikaga supremacy.
MURO MACHI	Onin 1 / Bummei 9	1467-77	Feudal Wars of Onin. Many families destroyed.
	Bummei 9	1477	Collapse of central government as result of civil war. Ashikaga Shoguns powerless. Imperial House penniless.
	Mei-o 9	1500	Whole of Japan at war. Many peasant uprisings.
	Tembun 11	1542	Contact with the West; three Portuguese shipwrecked. Traders and Jesuit priests follow.
SENGOKU	Tembun 18	1549	Spanish missionary St. Francis Xavier reaches Japan.
	Eiroku 11	1568	Nobunaga de facto Shogun; end of Ashikaga power.
	Genki 2	1571	Nobunaga destroys warlike monasteries and crushes Buddhism as a political force.
ADZUCHI-MOMOYAMA	Tensho 10	1582	Toyotomi Hideyoshi succeeds Nobunaga. Imposes peace.
	Tensho 15	1587	First Christian persecution.
	Bunroku 1	1592	Unsuccessful Korean expedition, terminated in 1598 by death of Hideyoshi.
	Keicho 2	1597	Second Korean expedition.
	Keicho 3	1598	Iyeyasu, founder of Tokugawa family, succeeds Hideyoshi.

MILITARY DICTATORSHIP exerting limited authority over feudal society. Decentralization and civil wars. Destruction of power of old families. Emergence of adventurer-dictators.

SOME SIGNIFICANT EVENTS IN JAPANESE HISTORY * — Continued

Chronology

Political Evolution	Japanese periods	Japanese dates	Western dates	Chronology
	Yedo	Keicho 5	1600	Battle of Sekigahara, won by Iyeyasu, against rebel chiefs. Yedo, later called Tokyo, becomes capital. Iyeyasu becomes Shogun.
		Genwa 1	1615	Iyeyasu becomes master of Japan by victory at Osaka Castle.
		Genwa 8 / Kenian 4	1622-51	Zenith of feudal institutions, under third Tokugawa Shogun, Iyemitsu.
		Kanei 1	1624	Expulsion of the Spaniards. Increasing anti-foreign feeling.
		Kanei 14	1637	Drastic anti-foreign and anti-Christian edict. Shimabara rebellion, primarily caused by agrarian troubles, but given moral impetus by Christianity, leads to expulsion of Portuguese and closure of country to foreign influence.
		Meireki 3	1657	Great fire in Yedo.
		Kyoho 1	1716	Increased pressure from changing economic conditions. Yoshimune, an enlightened Shogun, tries to remedy desperate situation by a "back to Iyeyasu" program. Relaxes bar against Western learning by allowing Dutch books to enter.
CENTRALIZED, SELF-ISOLATED, FEUDAL SYSTEM. Collapse of agricultural economy.		Tem-mei 3-7	1783-7	Rice riots. Attempted reforms of Matsudaira Sadanobu. Growing feeling against the shogunate.
Bankruptcy, social disintegration, and economic chaos. End of isolation.		Tempo 9	1838	Famines; financial embarrassment of shogunate; general economic collapse threatened.
		Kaei 6 / Ansei 1	1853-4	Perry's "black ships" arrive; first treaty with U. S. signed.
		Ansei 5	1858	Commercial treaty with U. S. signed without Emperor's sanction. Opposition to shogunate foments anti-foreign demonstration in which "outside lords," especially of Satsuma and Choshu, are leaders.
		Bunkyu 3	1863	Reprisal bombardment of Kagoshima, capital of Satsuma clan, by British fleet. American, Dutch, and French vessels fired on by Choshu forts at Shimonoseki.
		Ganji 1	1864	Reprisal movement of four powers. Choshu forts destroyed by allied squadron of Dutch, French, and British ships.

* Taken from *Fortune* magazine, September, 1936, issue.

286

	Period	Year	Event
INDUSTRIAL REVOLUTION imported. Feudalism ended. Power "restored" to Emperor under Constitution. (Meiji)	Keio 3 / Meiji 1	1867–8	Shogunate overthrown. "Restoration" of power to Emperor. Mutsuhito accedes as Emperor Meiji; moves to Yedo, names it Tokyo, "Eastern Capital."
	Meiji 2	1869	Chiefs of the four great clans (Satsuma, Choshu, Tosa, and Hizen) surrender their fiefs to the Emperor, clan heads made governors of former provinces.
	Meiji 4	1871	Second reorganization. System of local autonomy abolished. Disestablishment of samurai.
	Meiji 7	1874	First Popular Assembly. Alliance between government and Mitsubishi interests for punitive expedition against Formosa.
	Meiji 9	1876	Samurai forbidden to wear two swords. Conscript army of all classes set up. Dissatisfaction of samurai culminates in the Satsuma rebellion "not against the Emperor but against his evil counselors."
	Meiji 22	1889	Constitution (drafted by Prince Ito, on German model, after study of European forms of government) solemnly promulgated. Imperial Diet opened 1890.
Emergence of Japan as a WORLD POWER.	Meiji 27–28	1894–5	Sino-Japanese War, won by Japanese.
	Meiji 35	1902	Anglo-Japanese Treaty.
	Meiji 37–8	1904–5	Russo-Japanese War, won by Japanese.
	Meiji 38	1905	Anglo-Japanese Alliance.
	Meiji 43	1910	Korea annexed to Japan by imperial rescript.
	Meiji 44	1911	"Gentleman's Agreement," by which Japan voluntarily limits emigration to Canada and U. S.
(WORLD / TAISHO)	Taisho 1	1912	End of Meiji reign. Accession of Yoshihito.
	Taisho 3	1914	Japan enters the World War on the side of the Allies.
	Taisho 10	1921	Incapacity of Taisho. Regency of Hirohito.
	Taisho 12	1923	Great Earthquake.
	Taisho 13	1924	U. S. Congress passes exclusion law aimed at the Japanese.
(SHOWA)	Showa 1	1926	Death of Emperor Yoshihito. The Showa period begins with Emperor Hirohito.
	Showa 6	1931	The Manchurian Adventure.
	Showa 12	1937	War with China.
	Showa 16	1941	Attack on Pearl Harbor.
	Showa 19	1944	Japan is driven back.

SOME SIGNIFICANT EVENTS IN JAPANESE HISTORY—*Continued*

Political Evolution	Japanese periods	Japanese dates	Western dates	Chronology
Japan in defeat, occupation, and recovery.	Showa	Showa 20	1945	Japan is defeated and occupied.
		Showa 20–26	1945–52	Occupation by the Allied Powers.
		Showa 25	1951	The treaty of peace is signed in San Francisco.
		Showa 26	1952	The occupation ends.
		Showa 28	1954	Mutual Defense Assistance Agreement between Japan and the United States.

APPENDIX II

LIST OF READINGS

This list of readings is not meant to be exhaustive. An attempt has been made to name a few of the books which will prove useful to those who wish a more detailed treatment.

Far Eastern and Pacific Problems

K. S. Latourette, *A Short History of the Far East.* New York: The Macmillan Company, 3rd ed., 1957.

Japan

H. Borton, *Japan's Modern Century.* New York: The Ronald Press Company, 1955.

H. Borton, S. Eliséeff, W. W. Lockwood, J. C. Pelzel, *A Selected List of Books and Articles on Japan in English, French, and German.* Cambridge, Mass.: Harvard University Press, 1954.

R. Brines, *MacArthur's Japan.* Philadelphia: J. B. Lippincott Company, 1948.

D. M. Brown, *Nationalism in Japan: An Introductory Historical Analysis.* Berkeley, Calif.: University of California Press, 1955.

R. J. C. Butow, *Japan's Decision to Surrender.* Stanford, Calif.: Stanford University Press, 1954.

H. Byas, *Government by Assassination.* New York: Alfred A. Knopf, 1942.

C. D. Carus, *Japan: Its Resources and Industries.* New York: Harper & Brothers, 1944.

J. F. Embree, *Suye Mura: A Japanese Village.* Chicago: The University of Chicago Press, 1939.

H. Feis, *The Road to Pearl Harbor: The Coming of the War Between the United States and Japan.* Princeton: Princeton University Press, 1950.

F. Gibney, *Five Gentlemen of Japan.* New York: Farrar, Straus and Young, 1953.

J. C. Grew, *Ten Years in Japan.* New York: Simon and Schuster, 1944.

F. C. Jones, *Japan's New Order in East Asia, Its Rise and Fall*. New York: Oxford University Press, 1954.

T. Kase, *Journey to the Missouri*. New Haven: Yale University Press, 1950.

E. M. Martin, *The Allied Occupation of Japan*. New York: American Institute of Pacific Relations, 1948.

E. H. Norman, *Japan's Emergence as a Modern State: Political and Economic Problems of the Meiji Period*. New York: American Institute of Pacific Relations, 1940.

H. S. Quigley and J. E. Turner, *The New Japan; Government and Politics*. Minneapolis, Minn.: University of Minnesota Press, 1956.

E. O. Reischauer, *Japan, Past and Present*. New York: Alfred A. Knopf, 1946.

G. B. Sansom, *Japan, A Short Cultural History*. New York: Appleton-Century-Crofts, 1943.

G. B. Sansom, *The Western World and Japan: A Study in the Interaction of European and Asiatic Cultures*. New York: Alfred A. Knopf, 1949.

R. S. Schwantes, *Japanese and Americans: A Century of Cultural Relations*. New York: Harper & Brothers, 1955.

P. J. Treat, *Diplomatic Relations Between the United States and Japan*. 3 vols., Stanford, Calif.: Stanford University Press, 1932–1938.

G. T. Trewartha, *Japan: A Physical, Cultural, and Regional Geography*. Madison, Wis.: The University of Wisconsin Press, 1945.

C. Yanaga, *Japan Since Perry*. New York: McGraw-Hill Book Company, 1949.

INDEX

A

Aborigines, 11
Adaptability of Japanese, 65–6, 273
Administration, under American occupancy, 270–277
Agriculture, 12, 23, 54, 132, 195, 272
Ainu, 1, 4, 11, 12, 14, 34, 122
Air raids on Japan, 265, 268–9
Alaska, 80
Aleutian Islands, 81, 250, 262, 266
Allied Council for Japan, 270
America, *see* United States
Amoy, 249
Amphibious warfare, 259
Amur, 80, 123, 144, 168, 189
Anatomy, 80
Ancestor-worship, 15, 75
Anglo-Japanese Alliance, 145, 149–50, 165, 170
Annam, 49
Anti-Comintern Pact, 190, 233, 246–7
Antisubversive Activity Law, 280
Archery (illus.), 58
Architecture, 23, 26, 55, 66, 68; examples of (illus.), 32
Aristocracy, 97, 220
Arms Conference (London, 1930), 182, 215
Army, reorganized, 97; growing power of, 209–10, 213–21; (illus.) 264
Art, 8, 11, 13, 22–3, 30, 38–9, 54, 67–8
Asahi, newspaper, 228
Ashikaga Period, 39–44
Aso, Mt. (illus.), 7

B

Assam, 261, 267–8
Assassination, 107–8, 218–9
Australia, 176, 252, 259, 261, 266
Automobile, 176
Axis, 190, 233, 246–7, 248

B

Bakufu, 36–7, 46–8, 53, 56, 60, 78, 85, 88, 220
"Banditry," 186
Bank of Japan, 131
Banks, 99, 130–1
Baseball, 229
Bataan, 261
Bay of Bengal, 261
Birth control, 198, 281
Bismarck, 112
Black Current, 8
Blockade of China, 241
Bolshevist régime, 168
Bonin Islands, 122–3, 232, 269, 278
Books, 54, 229
Borneo, 248, 259
Boxer Rebellion, 143; Protocol, 236, 250
Boycotts, anti-Japanese, 166, 179, 180, 190, 250
Brussels conference, 249
Bryan, William J., 172
Buddhism, 17, 18–21, 30, 38, 42, 45, 51, 54, 56, 65–6, 72–4, 223, 224–6, 281
Buppo, 72
Bureaucracy, 64–5, 92, 98, 220
Burma, 40, 246, 249, 261, 263, 265, 278
Burma Road, 246, 252, 261, 265
Bushi, 34